WESTERN CANON LAW

WESTERN
CANON LAW

BY

R. C. MORTIMER, D.D.

LORD BISHOP OF EXETER

SOMETIME LECTURER IN EARLY CANON LAW
IN THE UNIVERSITY OF OXFORD

LONDON
ADAM AND CHARLES BLACK

FIRST PUBLISHED 1953
A. AND C. BLACK LIMITED
4, 5 AND 6 SOHO SQUARE, LONDON W.1

MADE IN GREAT BRITAIN
PRINTED BY THE BOWERING PRESS, PLYMOUTH

PREFACE

THESE lectures were given on the Berkeley campus of the University of California in the Spring of 1951. The Church Divinity School of the Pacific first invited me to lecture to students at the school: the invitation won the support of the Law School at the University, and through the active interest of Dean William L. Prosser and of Mr. Vernon Smith, the Librarian, the University Committee on Drama, Lectures and Music was persuaded to arrange for the lectures to be delivered within the precincts of the University under the joint sponsorship of the Church Divinity School of the Pacific and the Law School. The generosity of my friend Dr. Lloyd Robbins of San Francisco enabled me to accept the invitation and to enjoy the exhilaration of addressing an American audience. It is to him, therefore, that I dedicate this book in gratitude for the many kindnesses which he has done me. And I would take this opportunity of expressing my thanks to the University of California for the privilege of having been allowed the use of a lecture room, and to the audience which endured the lectures.

The lectures contain a broad outline of the development of canon law in Western Christendom down to the Reformation. I have deliberately omitted any account of the parallel development in the East. I have done this because my pre-occupation is with the Church of England and the Anglican Communion. Upon the Church of England Eastern canon law has had no effective impact, except for the inclusion in the Penitentials of certain Eastern characteristics, perhaps under the influence of Archbishop Theodore. The Church of England developed with the development of Western Christendom, and it is in the Western canon law that her own canon law is rooted. To the historical sketch of

the first three lectures I have added, in the fourth, a brief account of what has happened to the canon law in England since the Reformation; what of it remains and what of it has passed out of use, and the hopes and intentions of the Revision which is now being attempted. Finally I have added some reflections of my own on the peculiar nature of the canon law, on some of the ways in which it differs from other systems of jurisprudence, and on some of the principles which ecclesiastical legislators ought always to bear in mind.

My main purpose in writing these lectures has been to provide for Anglican Ordination candidates in particular and for the Anglican clergy and laity in general, an introduction to the study of this important subject. It is my hope to do something to remove that neglect and ignorance of canon law which has, in my judgement, been a source of grave weakness to the Church of England in the latter part of her history. Yet, I hope also that these lectures may be of some use to members of other Christian denominations as well.

It will be noticed that I have assumed, and have made no attempt to prove the authority of the Church to legislate for her members. If that authority be denied the canon law itself is, of course, demolished and has but a fictional existence. It will further be noticed that I have not attempted a definition of the Church. To have done so would have involved me in a discussion of denominational differences and would have thrown the whole course of the lectures out of balance. For the same reason I have not defined where in the Church the legislative authority lies. This would have involved a discussion of the claims of the Papacy (and of the Episcopacy and of the Presbytery) with the same result.

Lastly I must acknowledge the extensive use which I have made of the great work on the Canonical Collections by Fournier and Le Bras,[1] and of an American book on the Penitentials.[2] Without the help of these books I could not

[1] Histoire des Collections Canoniques en Occident. Fournier et Le Bras. (Paris, 1932.)

[2] Mediaeval Handbooks of Penance. McNeill and Gamer. (Columbia University, 1938.)

have written the lectures at all. My own personal knowledge and study is too limited to certain particular periods and subjects.

These lectures are introductory only. Those whom they may tempt to pursue the subject further I refer to the short bibliography printed at the end.

ROBERT EXON:

CONTENTS

THE GROWTH OF THE CLASSICAL TRADITION

THE word "canon" meant, originally, a straight rod or line, something by which you measure; and so a definite rule. It is applied to creeds, which are the rules of faith, its defined content by reference to which heresy can be measured. It is applied to the books of the Bible; for they fall within the line drawn by the Church and so are those which the rule of the Church recognises as portions of Holy Scripture. It is applied to the clergy, who fall within the line and so are on the list. For many centuries now it has been applied in this sense only to those clergy who are on the list of a Cathedral; but in Patristic times it was applied to all the clergy on the list of a Bishop. The commonest application of the word, for us, is to the definitions or rules drawn up and agreed upon by a Council. In its strictest sense canon law means laws or canons passed by councils. It came, as we shall see, to include a great deal else beside, but in origin and strictly speaking, canon law is the law contained in canons. And canons define and determine the organisation of the Church and the conduct and duties of its members. They set forth the norm or standard in these matters accepted and expected by the Church.

Canon law may be said to have begun with the Council of Nicaea in the year 325. Not that there were not earlier councils which also passed canons—there were, for example, councils in Africa, under Cyprian in the third century which decided what was to be done with Christians who broke down under persecution but afterwards repented. And there was the famous Council of Arles in 314 which was attended by two delegates from England and at which it was finally decided that no individual may ever be baptised twice. But the Council of Nicaea is the first oecumenical council, and

the first council whose canons were everywhere received with respect and regarded as binding throughout the whole of Christendom. For many hundreds of years the canons of Nicaea find their place in all collections of canon law as items of supreme and unquestioned authority. Indeed, so great was their authority that in the early Middle Ages they were, together with the canons of the later oecumenical councils, put on a level with Scripture as being unalterable and admitting of no exceptions.

The canons of Nicaea were, of course, originally written in Greek, but they were early translated into Latin. Two such Latin versions, at least, belong to the fourth century and one of them, that of Caecilian, may be contemporary, and the official version which that bishop brought back with him from Nicaea to Carthage. These Nicene canons appear to have formed the beginning, the first section, of all the earliest collections of canons or church law-books. Their importance, the respect and veneration in which they were held is perhaps best illustrated by "the affair of Apiarius".

Apiarius was an African cleric who early in the fifth century was degraded and excommunicated by the Church of Africa. It is not clear on what grounds. Apiarius left Africa, made his way to Italy and there appealed to the Pope. The Pope heard his case and wrote to the African bishops. The African bishops were most indignant and protested that Apiarius had no right to appeal to a "foreign" bishop, nor the Pope any right to hear such an appeal. The Pope replied that he was acting in accordance with the canons of Nicaea, one of which explicitly provided for such an appeal, and he enclosed a copy of the Nicene canons so that they could see for themselves. The African bishops met in council at Carthage in 419. They looked at the Pope's copy of the canons of Nicaea and there, sure enough, was a canon authorising an appeal to Rome. They then looked at their own copy, preserved in the archives of the Church of Carthage—probably the very copy which Caecilian, Bishop of Carthage, had brought back with him from Nicaea in 325. In that copy no such canon appeared.

They wrote and told the Pope this, but added that if it should turn out that the African copy of the Nicene canons was defective, and that the Pope's version was correct, they would, of course, acquiesce and act in obedience to the rulings of the holy and oecumenical synod of Nicaea. Meanwhile they were writing to the great churches of Constantinople and Alexandria to enquire whether the disputed canon appeared in the versions of those churches. In due course they heard that the canon was not in the version of either church. The Africans, accordingly, stood their ground.

In fact, the canon was one of the canons of a council held at Sardica in 341. I have told this story at some length partly in order to illustrate the tremendous prestige attaching to the Nicene canons, and partly to show the way in which the earliest collections of canons were made. For how did the Pope come to make this extraordinary mistake of attributing a canon of Sardica to the Council of Nicaea? The explanation is very simple. In the Roman version of the canons of Nicaea the canons of Sardica were added on in a single numbered series. There are still extant some manuscripts which do this and which indicate that the earlier manuscripts of which they are copies did. So to attribute all the canons of Sardica to the Council of Nicaea was a very easy and natural mistake.

This tacking the canons of one council on to those of another was the usual early way of compiling a church law-book. You took the canons of such councils as you knew and numbered them off in a single series from one to a hundred and fifty, or whatever the number might be. Generally, though as the Roman example has just showed us not always, you indicated by a rubric or a short preamble where each new council began. The first collection of this kind of which we know is a small Pontic collection. It consists of the canons of three councils held in Pontus in the early fourth century; they are Ancyra, Neo-Caesarea and Gangra. To them are prefaced the canons of Nicaea. Still in the fourth century this collection was enlarged by the canons of Antioch (341)

and of Laodicea (345). This small and early collection was of
sufficient importance to be used officially as a law-book at
the oecumenical council of Chalcedon in 451. In the minutes
of that council it is recorded that in the fourth session "canons
83 and 84" were read. But canons 83 and 84 as there set out
are canons 4 and 5 of the Council of Antioch. Again in
Session eleven it is said that canons 95 and 96 were read.
Canons 95 and 96 are the sixteenth and seventeenth canons
of Antioch. The numbers are of course the numbers of the
one continuous series of the whole collection. This collection
was soon translated into Latin and circulated widely in the
West; it was so popular that several different translations
were made. It was later enlarged by the addition of the
translated canons of the two oecumenical councils of Constantinople and Chalcedon, and the canons of Sardica were
inserted immediately after those of Nicaea.

Here, then, we have the beginnings of canon law strictly
so called. First the law-book, in all probability, of the great
church of Constantinople, this same book is enlarged and
adapted to suit the Church of Rome. In much the same way
the church in Africa built up its own canon law. As the
council of Chalcedon opened with a ratification of the canons
of previous councils, and possibly with a reading of them—
much as we now open a meeting with a reading of the minutes
of the previous meeting—so it seems to have been the practice
in Africa to begin a council by reading and confirming the
canons of earlier synods. Thus it is that in the records of the
Council of Carthage held in 419 there is preserved for us a
long series of canons of earlier councils. This is often known
as "The African Codex". There is an interesting and important piece of work waiting to be done in the preparation
of an edited text of this codex. The main source is the Codex
of Dionysius, to which I shall come in a moment: but this
needs to be conflated with other streams of tradition and
enlarged with the addition of some other extant material.
The whole needs to be annotated.

No doubt the other great churches formed similar early

collections—Alexandria, for example, and Antioch, Milan, Arles in Gaul. We are very ignorant of their nature, and even in some cases of their existence. They would have contained different blocks of material, some of general and some of local interest. You would expect to find in them the canons of the Greek councils to which I have already referred, those of Sardica, perhaps some from Africa or Gaul, a Papal decretal or two relating to some controversy in which the church or region in question had itself been involved, and a series of canons of local councils. In fact, you would look for the kind of documents naturally preserved in the archives of an important church.

Such in fact was the material, chaotic and variable, which the first great canonist known to us by name found in the archives of the most important church of them all. Somewhere about the year 500 Dionysius Exiguus, a Scythian monk, produced in Rome a collection of canons. It contains just what we should expect—the canons of the Greek councils of Nicaea, Ancyra, Neo-Caesarea, Gangra, Antioch, Laodicea, Constantinople and Chalcedon. Of these, Dionysius says in his Preface, he has himself made new and accurate translations from copies of the Greek originals. The collection also contains the canons of Sardica and of the first session of the Council of Carthage, 419. At the beginning Dionysius put a translation, which he made himself, of the first fifty of the so-called Apostolic canons—an apocryphal work of the fourth century. Dionysius did not himself believe that these canons were of apostolic origin, but he included them because they contain some very clear and important provisions, and because they had been quoted in some of the Papal Letters. This first edition of the collection of Dionysius is preserved in a single manuscript which has been edited by A. Strewe (Berlin, 1931).

Very soon after its publication Dionysius issued a second edition. In this he included the full records of the Council of Carthage 419, and so preserved for us "The African Codex". He also re-numbered the canons, with a separate series of

numbers for each council. A few years later he published a collection of 39 Decretals of different Popes, from Siricius (384–98) to Anastasius II (496–8). The bulk of these decretals, 21 in all, belong to Innocent the Great. From this time onwards the decrees of the Popes play an ever-increasing part in Western Canon Law.

Though, as we shall see, the two books of Dionysius, known together as the Dionysiana, have a lasting place of profound importance in the development of the canon law, they were not the only products of this particular period. During this Indian Summer of the Western Empire, when the Ostro-Goth Theodoric reigned in Italy and Gelasius was Pope, others besides Dionysius produced similar collections of canons and decretals. Some are still extant, e.g. the Freising, the Vatican, the S. Blaise and the Chieti Collections, to give them the names by which they are now commonly known to scholars. Composed in Rome or thereabouts their influence spread all over North Italy and across the Alps into Gaul. With the Dionysiana supreme amongst them they constitute a large part of that classical canon law, which through the medium of the collection of Dionysius became the norm or standard to which the canon law in the course of its development was constantly returning. Yet these collections were very far from perfect.

In the first place they differed among themselves in their content. Though they have much in common, each also makes its individual contribution with a further set of councils or a different collection of decretals. They have a varying standard of accuracy in the chronological arrangement of their material; for the arrangement is, in the main, chronological, and no attempt is made to order the material according to subject matter; and there is a good deal of overlapping. It is a tedious business to collect from their many hiding-places each several item dealing with a particular matter. Further, even in the matter which they have in common they use different translations of Greek originals and this could result in a wide diversity of interpretation. Perhaps it

it worth while to give as an illustration the different versions of Canon 6 of Nicaea.[1]

Dionysius, accurately translating the Greek, has for title, "Of the privileges which belong to certain cities" and the first few lines of the text run, "Let the ancient custom be maintained throughout Egypt, Libya and Pentapolis, that the Bishop of Alexandria has authority over them all, because there is a similar custom in the case of the Bishop of Rome: similarly with Antioch and the other provinces, let the churches retain their privileges." Now "The Prisca" version runs thus: "Of the primacy of the Church of Rome and the bishops of other cities. There is an ancient custom that the Bishop of the city of Rome has an overlordship so that he governs the neighbouring (suburban) regions and the whole province. The Bishop of Alexandria has authority throughout Egypt. Similarly with Antioch and in the other provinces let the metropolitan churches retain their proper privileges." "The Ingilram" version (Chieti) reads: "Of the Primacy of the Church of Rome: The Church of Rome has ever had a primacy. Let Egypt also have it so that the Bishop of Alexandria has authority over all, since the Roman bishop has this custom. Similarly also with the bishop in Antioch: and in the other provinces let the churches of the greater cities have a primacy." These are the two extreme deviations from or amplifications of the original text. But there are four or five intermediate forms of texts. So it can be readily understood how difficult it was to be sure of the original meaning or to avoid conflicting interpretations.

Soon after the appearance of these collections of the ancient law Western Europe entered the Dark Ages. Of the confusion and corruption occasioned by this I shall have something to say in the next lecture. It is enough to say here that the old law was either ignored in anarchy, or overlaid by new local customs, or corrupted by Irish and Anglo-Saxon influences.

---

[1] Further study of these collections is badly needed: a beginning may be made from a study of the MSS. sources furnished by Maassen's monumental work *Geschichte der Quellen und der Literatur der canonischen Rechts im Abendlande bis zum Angange der Mittelalters.*

B

Only in Spain was there a sort of golden age in the development of canon law. This culminated in the formation of the
great collection known as the Hispana. The Hispana is the
twin-pillar with the code of Dionysius of the whole structure
of the classical canon law. In its earliest form it dates from 633.
It contains a preface, index, the Greek councils, the African
councils, 10 Gallican councils, 14 Spanish councils and 104
Decretals. It was later added to by the inclusion of some
further Gallican councils and of the complete series of Spanish
councils down to and including the seventeenth of Toledo
in 694. It is an admirable collection, far fuller than that of
Dionysius—for it has, as Dionysius has not, the Gallican and
Spanish councils, and gives us 104 Decretals against the 39 of
Dionysius. The material is drawn from excellent sources and
admirably arranged chronologically by countries or by
cities. But it was, of course, difficult to handle, precisely because of the wealth of its material. What was needed was a
re-arrangement of its content according to subject matter.
At some time, apparently, in the second half of the seventh
century this was done. A Table was drawn up in ten books.
Each book was sub-divided into Chapters; in each chapter
are collected, in the same order as in the Hispana, all the
texts and canons dealing with the particular matter with
which the chapter is concerned. The titles of the books are
worth giving because they exercised considerable influence
on the arrangement of later collections, and because they
give some idea of the subject-matter with which the Hispana
deals. They are:

1. Ordination, Orders, the life of the Clergy.
2. Monks, nuns, widows, public penitents.
3. Church courts, trials, accusations, etc., councils, church
    property.
4. Liturgy, Baptism.
5. Marriage, sins of the flesh, murder.
6. Duties and moral conduct of clergy and of laity.
7. The Crown.

8. Theological questions.
9. Heresy.
10. Idolatry, Apostasy.

We return now to Gaul. There, the middle of the eighth century found the Church a prey to spoliation from outside, to decadence and vice inside and with her legal and administrative system in confusion. It is a time of anarchy and chaos. The connection with Rome and Italy has been weakened, the provincial organisation has been gravely impaired by the erection of small kingdoms whose frontiers cut across those of the old provinces and even divided up dioceses. The regular meetings of bishops in Synod, which had been a feature of French life in the first half of the sixth century and which gave rise to a rich series of canons and collections—we have seen them make their appearance in the Hispana—had disappeared, and each bishop ruled his diocese in isolation, and observed such rules as he wished. Moreover, the quality of the bishops had deteriorated. Kings and nobles regarded the property of the Church as their own, they kept the sees vacant for long periods, and then gave them to their kindred or dependants. The old rules about election and consecration went by the board. The bishops thus appointed were more at home on the battlefield or out hunting than in their churches. As with the bishops so too, naturally, with their clergy. They were ordained without proper scrutiny, and often lacked both faith and morals. Themselves no example of holy living to their people, the laity were abandoned to every kind of vice. Thus on the external organisational side of Church life, there was everywhere an ignoring of the old rules of the canon law.

This was the situation which the movement known as the Carolingian reform attempted to correct. It's aims were to reorganise the hierarchy, to restore discipline among the clergy and laity and to recover ecclesiastical property from the lay hands into which much of it had fallen. The parties to this reforming movement were the Popes, the Bishops and

the Carolingian Emperors. Their first move was to restore
the old canon law, the provisions of which were now almost
forgotten. To this end it was necessary to have an authentic
and authoritative collection of the pure ancient law, free of
all local corruption and embodying beyond all doubt the
true discipline of the Church. They sought for such a collection, naturally enough, in Rome. There in 774 Charlemagne
received at the hands of Pope Hadrian an enlarged edition
of the old code of Dionysius. It is known as the Hadriana.
The enlargement consists mainly of fifteen extracts from
Decretals or Roman synods. Charlemagne took this collection back with him to Gaul and caused the Gallican church
officially to receive it at a council held at Aix-la-Chapelle
in 802. With this collection in their hands the French bishops
could see how wide a gulf separated the present condition of
the French Church from the ancient discipline. And with
the aid of this collection they set about the task of discredit-
ing and denouncing the various abuses which had crept in
and the councils, books or individuals responsible for them.

But the Hadriana was not in itself sufficient for this purpose.
It did not cover a wide enough ground. Accordingly they
brought in to their assistance the much larger Hispana collection. With the combination of the Hadriana and the
Hispana the reformers had all the material which they
needed. The two collections in fact overlap, and what
actually happened was that the Hadriana was used as a
source for the Greek councils, the Hispana as a source for
the rest. Through the alliance of these two great collections,
the ancient law secured a firm and unshakeable place in the
body of canon law.

It will be convenient to interrupt at this point this short
historical sketch of the development of Western canon law
in order to describe briefly the nature and content of this
ancient law. This is, in my judgement, a matter of supreme
importance. For this ancient law contains the fundamental
principles of Church Order. I believe that a close study of
this law will greatly help us all to a better understanding of

the nature of the Church, and even that the way to Re-
union, ultimately, lies in a return to these principles where
they have been abandoned, denied or forgotten. Certainly,
I think, that any scholar who would present to the modern
world a carefully analysed and annotated account of the
content of this law would render a service of the greatest
practical advantage and benefit.

Perhaps the easiest way of indicating roughly the nature
of this law and the kind of matters with which it deals would
be to summarise shortly the canons of three Greek councils,
one Decretal and one Gallican council. These are the Canons
of Nicaea: (1) Of those who castrate themselves. (They are
not to be ordained.) (2) Of the newly baptised. (They are not
to be ordained immediately.) (3) Of the kind of woman who
may be allowed to live in the same house as the clergy (i.e.
of clerical housekeepers). (4) Of the election and consecration of bishops. (Elected by all bishops of the province:
consecrated by at least three: the Metropolitan confirms.)
(5) Of persons excommunicated. (A man excommunicated
by one bishop is not to be absolved by another.) Provision of
an appeal from the Bishop to the Synod. (6) Of the privileges which belong to certain sees. (7) Position of Bishop of
Jerusalem. (8) Of the Puritans (i.e. Novatianists) conditions
of re-union and reception. (9) Of the careless ordination of
unworthy priests. (To be deposed.) (10–14) Treatment of
different classes of lapsed Christians. (15) Transference of
clergy from one diocese to another forbidden. (16) The same,
plus prohibition of a bishop's ordaining a man from another
diocese. (17) Clergy are not to practise usury. (18) Of the
privileges of the priesthood. (A liturgical canon dealing with
duties and demeanour of the grades of the hierarchy in the
Eucharist.) (19) Of Paulianists: conditions of re-union and
reception. (20) No kneeling in church at Easter-tide.

The Canons of Neo-Caesarea: (1) Priests not to marry.
(2) No marriage with deceased husband's brother. (3) None
to marry often. (4) No penance for intention (unfulfilled) to
commit adultery. (5) Treatment of catechumens who com-

mit grave sins. (6) Women with child may be baptised.
(7) Clergy not to take part in the celebration of second marriages. (8) Adulterous wife bars a man from ordination: if he
is already ordained, he must separate from her. (9) Priests
guilty of grave sin before ordination to be suspended. (10)
Deacons: the same. (11) None to be ordained priest under
thirty. (12) A man baptised because it was thought he was
going to die is, as a rule, ineligible for ordination. (13) The
inferior status of parochial clergy. (14) Each diocese to have
seven deacons.

The Canons of Antioch: (1) Nicene regulations about how
to calculate the date of Easter to be observed. (2) Against
schismatics, and those who join with them. (3) Against clergy
who migrate to another diocese without leave. (4) Against
clergy who dare to minister after being excommunicated.
(5) Against schismatics. (6) A man excommunicated by one
bishop is not to be received by another: provision of an
appeal to a synod. (7) Provisions for strangers to be received
in church only if they have commendatory letters. (9) The
authority of metropolitans: and of diocesan bishops. (10) Of
the limited powers of "country bishops". (11 and 12) Appeals
to the State: must be authorised by metropolitan or council.
(13) Bishops not to ordain outside their own provinces.
(14) Provision for a bishop to be tried by the Synod and
neighbouring bishops to be called in if necessary. (15) No
appeal from a unanimous verdict. (16) Election of bishops.
(17 and 18) Of non-resident bishops. (19) Of the consecration of a bishop. (20) Two synods to be held every year. (21)
No translation of bishops. (22) Bishops not to ordain in the
dioceses of other bishops. (23) Bishops not to appoint their
own successors. (28 and 29) Church property: the Bishop to
administer.

The letter of Innocent to Victricius. (1) Election of a
bishop requires consultation with the Metropolitan: his consecration requires more than one bishop. (2) Soldiers are
ineligible for ordination. Disputes between clergy are to be
settled by the provincial synod. No appeal except to Rome,

as laid down at Sardica. (3) None in minor orders to marry a widow. (4) A layman marrying a widow is ineligible for ordination. (5) None who marry twice are eligible for ordination. (5) No bishop to ordain anyone belonging to another diocese. (6) Heretics not to be re-baptised. (7) The higher clergy are not to co-habit with their wives. (8) Monks taking orders are not exempt from their vows. (9) Officers of state and civil servants are not to be ordained, because their official duties raise complications for a clergyman. (10) Nuns who break their vow of chastity are to be excommunicated. (11) Women, not being nuns, who have made a private vow of chastity and break it may be admitted to penance.

The Statuta Ecclesiae Antiqua. This collection of 104 canons is called, in the Hispana, the fourth Council of Carthage. There is no doubt, however, that it is in fact Gallican, and dates, probably, from the time of Caesarius, Bishop of Arles—early sixth century. Canons 1–10 are liturgical and give instructions for the manner of ordaining to all ranks of the clergy from Bishop to Cantor. (12) Widows and nuns to prepare women for baptism. (14) The Bishop to keep a guest-house near the church. (15) The Bishop to live simply, and (16) not to read pagan books. (17) If a guardian to orphans, etc., to act through the archdeacon. (18) Not to act as executor of wills. (19) Not to go to law. (20) To spend his time in prayer and reading. (21) To attend the synod in person, or by delegate. (22) Not to ordain without consulting his clergy and without the approval of the laity. (23) Not to hear accusations without the presence of his clergy. (24) No-one to leave church during the sermon. (27) Translations and preferments grudgingly allowed. (28–30) Conduct of trials. (31–32) Church property is held by the Bishop in trust, and is to be administered with the help of the clergy. (33) Visiting clergy are to be invited to preach and to celebrate. (36) A deacon may give communion if necessary. (44) The clergy cut their hair but do not shave. (45–50) Proper clerical behaviour. (51–53) Clergy are to earn their livings by handicrafts or by farming. (54—62) Quarrelsome and indecorous

clergy. (64) No fasting on Sunday. (65) Easter to be kept on the proper day. (67–69) Offences which bar from ordination. (74–82) Administration of penance. (84) Anybody—heretic or Jew—may attend the Mass of Catechumens. (85) Baptism is to be received fasting. (87) No recourse by Christians to pagan courts. (88) Going to games instead of Church on Sundays—excommunication. (89) Excommunication for sorcerers. (90–92) Exorcisms. (94–95) Offerings to the Church from unworthy persons to be refused. (99–100) Women not to teach in Church or baptise. (101–103) Maintenance of widows.

There are, of course, in these ancient canons many details which the lapse of centuries has made obsolete, undesirable or unenforceable. All the regulations regarding public penance, for instance, have nothing but historic interest for us. The condemnation of widows and widowers marrying again it is not desirable to revive. The western development which insisted upon strict clerical celibacy is more open to debate, as is the general prohibition of marriage after ordination. The requirement that the bishop remain the bishop of the See to which he is consecrated and that he be not allowed to be translated to another See is, I understand, the law of the Protestant Episcopal Church in America. It might be well to enforce it elsewhere in the Anglican Communion: though the advantage to the Church of some degree of flexibility is undeniable. But it is not to the details of the ancient law that I would call attention, but to its general structure and broad content. Here are laid the foundations of Church Order. Here are established customs and provisions which have been so much part and parcel of Church life that we tend to take them too easily for granted.

The organisation of the Church into dioceses and provinces is clearly established. The rights and duties of a bishop within his diocese are prescribed, as are his relations with his fellow-bishops. The way in which bishops are to be elected is laid down, the assistance of the clergy and the consent of the laity therein are demanded: the rights and duties of

metropolitans in this respect are set out. There are rules concerning the creation of new Sees. There are many canons concerned with the qualities which are to be demanded in candidates for ordination. It is required that men be ordained only after due examination, and that they pass through the various grades of the hierarchy. Once ordained they are subject to their bishop, minister by his leave, and depart to another diocese only with his consent. A high standard of morality is demanded of them, and if they fail they are to be degraded. By means of regular synods the dioceses are to act in harmony with one another. Those whom one bishop excommunicates, other bishops are not to receive; but on appeal, all the bishops together in synod shall judge. The great churches—Rome, Constantinople, Antioch, etc.—occupy positions of special authority, yet this is based not on precise jurisdiction, but on veneration and prestige. The principle that Church matters and disputes between churchmen are to be settled in Church courts is sharply defined, and the general procedure in such matters—who are to judge and who may accuse and so forth—is laid down. The prohibition of marriage after divorce and within certain degrees of kinship finds frequent expression. The requirements for the due administration of the Sacraments of Baptism, Confirmation, Penance and the Eucharist are constantly stated.

Though the various collections in which this law is contained are not always in agreement with each other in every detail, though indeed there are inconsistencies and contradictions within each collection itself, nevertheless there emerges from these ancient codes a fairly clear picture of an ordered Church life; ordered in the relationship of province and diocese to each other, ordered in the selection and consecration of the Ministry, ordered in the several duties of the varied ranks of the clergy and of the laity, ordered in the administration of the Sacraments. I repeat that a closer study of this ancient law will be amply repaid in a deeper and clearer understanding of what the Church is.

CHAOS AND REFORM

THE Carolingian reforms had two objects. The first was to
check and correct the external abuses in the life and organisation of the Church which had been caused by the widespread
disregard of the provisions of the classical canon law. The
second was to counter a corruption and confusion which had
entered into the canon law itself. This corruption was due to
the well-intentioned efforts of the British Isles to reform and
educate the savage manners of the Dark Ages. The instrument of these efforts was a series of books known as the
Penitentials. With the Penitentials an entirely new element
enters into the stream of the canon law, and it is necessary for
us to examine them for a moment.

The Penitentials originate in the Celtic lands of Wales and
Ireland. Thence they spread to England and later to France
and Germany and even Italy. The Celtic Church was distinguished from every other part of Christendom by the
extent to which its organisation depended not on provinces
and dioceses, but on monastic houses and settlements. Its
penitential system seems to have grown out of the methods
and rules developed for the disciplining of monastic communities. The old canon law dealt only with the administration of
public penance. This was an elaborate and arduous discipline imposed upon those who confessed or were convicted
of grave sin. Like baptism it could be undergone only once
in a life-time, and it involved many life-long disabilities. It
is a matter of dispute whether any other penance than this
public penance was known to the early church.[1] Whatever
the truth of this may be, it is certain that private penance
lay almost entirely, if not entirely, outside the purview of the

---

[1] I would refer the reader to the writings of B. Poschman, E. Goller, P.
Galtier, and to my own book *The Origins of Private Penance.*

canon law. With the appearance of the Irish Penitentials this completely changed.

The Penitentials are handbooks for priests, by means of which they can, first, help those who come to make their confession to examine their consciences. They contain a series of questions or a list of sins. It seems that the priest was expected to read these over to the penitent. The danger of such a practice, in putting ideas into people's heads, is obvious. On the other hand, since a penalty, and a heavy penalty at that, was attached to each sin, the practice may well have had a severely discouraging effect. In the second place, the Penitentials were intended to help and instruct the confessor. They gave him a clear indication of the relative gravity of different sins and suggested an appropriate penance. Whatever the result may have been, the intention was that by the use of one of these books the confessor should be saved from sheer individualism and should deal with every type of sin in accordance with a recognised and respected authority.

There is much to be said in defence of the Penitentials. There are also many grave charges to be brought against them. In defence of them it must be admitted, first, that they exercised a strong civilising influence upon the barbarous Celts and Anglo-Saxons for whom they were first devised in the sixth century, and later upon the French and Germans. Murder, sexual vice, drunkenness, witch-craft, nature-worship, all the degrading features of barbaric life were the object of severe penances. I give examples from the First Book of the Penitential of Theodore. Chapter IV, paragraph 1, (p. 187)[1] is an attempt to check blood-feuds: "If one slays a man in revenge for a relative, he shall do penance as a murderer for seven or ten years. However, if he will render to the relatives the legal price, the penance shall be lighter, that is, it shall be shortened by half the time." Chapter II, paragraph 16, (p. 186): "If one commits fornication with

---

[1] The page references are to *Medieval Handbooks of Penance*. (McNeill and Gamer.)

his mother he shall do penance for 15 years. . . ." Chapter I, paragraph 3, (p. 184): "If a presbyter vomits on account of drunkenness, he shall do penance for forty days." Paragraph 5, (p. 184): "If a layman, he shall do penance for fifteen days." Chapter XV, paragraph 5, (p. 198): "If a woman puts her daughter upon a roof or into an oven for the cure of a fever, she shall do penance for seven years." Paragraph 4, (p. 198): "If a woman performs diabolical incantations or divinations she shall do penance for one year. . . ."

Secondly, the Penitentials contain a number of hygienic regulations which must similarly have exercised a civilising influence. For instance, in *The Irish Canons* (p. 118 ff.) we have penances inflicted for eating horseflesh, flesh which dogs have been eating, flesh of a dead beast: and for drinking liquids contaminated by a dog, eagle, crow, blackbird, cock or hen, cat or carcass of a beast. In these two ways, therefore, the Penitentials greatly assisted the secular government in promoting ordered, peaceful and civilised living.

Thirdly, the Penitentials afford evidence of a genuine desire to promote the spiritual life. They aim not merely at the suppression of vice, but also at the awakening of genuine repentance and the inculcation of positive virtues. For example, in *The Tripartite of S. Gall* we read in the Preface, "No priest or pontiff can treat the wounds of sinners or take away the sins from their souls unless in view of the pressing necessity he brings solicitude and prayers and tears. Therefore it is needful for us to be solicitous on behalf of sinners, since we are 'members one of another' and 'if one member suffers anything all the members suffer with it.' And, therefore, if we see anyone fallen in sin, let us also make haste to call him to penance by our teaching." (p. 283.)

Again, we find constant exhortations to the suppression of anger, e.g. The Penitential of Cummean:

"He who, justly or unjustly, makes his brother sad shall mollify by a satisfaction the rancor he has conceived, and so he shall be able to pray.

But if it is impossible to be reconciled with him, then at least he shall do penance, his priest being judge.

He who refuses to be reconciled shall live on bread and water for as long a time as he has been implacable.

He who hates his brother shall go on bread and water as long as he has not overcome his hatred; and he shall be joined to him whom he hates in sincere charity." (Chapter IV, paragraphs 1–4, p. 107.)

Sins of thought and intention, though properly regarded as less grave than actually perpetrated crimes, are yet treated severely, e.g. The Penitential of Cummean:

"He who loves in mind only, seven days.

"He who merely desires in his mind to commit fornication, but is not able, shall do penance for one year, especially in the three forty-day periods." (Chapter II, paragraphs 20 and 11, p. 104.)

Or the Paris Penitential: "If anyone keeps in his breast anger with another, he shall be judged a murderer; if he will not be reconciled to his brother whom he holds in hatred, he shall do penance on bread and water until such time as he is reconciled to him." (Paragraph 59, p. 280.)

Sin is regarded as a disease, and the penances imposed are spoken of as medicine, or as a system of treatment by which the disease can be cured. However mechanically the books may have been used in practise, in theory the confessor is constantly exhorted to treat each case on its merits, to distinguish between the varying rank and condition of different sinners, and to make allowance for ignorance or sudden temptation. It will be sufficient to quote from the Preface of the Penitential accredited to Bede:

"For not all are to be weighed in one and the same balance, although they be associated in one fault, but there shall be discrimination for each of these, that is: between rich and poor; freeman, slave; little child, boy, youth, young man, old man; stupid, intelligent; layman, cleric, monk; bishop, presbyter, deacon, subdeacon, reader, ordained or unordained; married or unmarried; pilgrim, virgin, canoness,

or nuns; the weak, the sick, the well. He shall make a distinction for the character of the sins or of the men; a continent person or one who is incontinent, wilfully or by accident; (whether the sin is committed) in public or in secret;
with what degree of compunction he (the culprit) makes
amends by necessity or by intention; the places and times
(of offences)." (p. 223.)

In this way casuistry and moral theology found their way
into canon law.

Yet however good their intentions, and however beneficial
their civilising effects, there are grave charges to be brought
against the Penitentials. In the first place there is the be-
wildering diversity of penances imposed for the same offences.
The books do not agree with each other or even sometimes
with themselves. The confessor is left to choose what penalty
he will. For example, the Penitential of Theodore states in
Chapter IV, paragraph 3 (p. 187): "But a murderer, ten or
seven years." And again in Chapter IV, paragraph 2 (p. 187):
"If one slays a man in revenge for a brother he shall do
penance for three years. In another place it is said that he
shall do penance for ten years." To the penitent it must have
made a difference which alternative the confessor chose.

Secondly, in some very important matters the Penitentials came into open conflict with the old discipline. For example, we find in Theodore an order to re-baptise those who
have been baptised by a priest guilty of fornication. Book 2,
Chapter II, paragraph 12, (p. 200). Again, marriage after
divorce is allowed in certain cases, e.g. after five years'
desertion, or if the wife is carried away prisoner; and the
wife also may marry again. More striking still, a man may
divorce his adulterous wife and marry again; and the wife,
too, after five years, may marry again. Book 2, Chapter XII,
paragraphs 5, 20–25, (pp. 208, 210). Again, the Penitentials
have a different rule about the prohibited degrees of kindred
and affinity.

Lastly, the Penitentials are open to a charge of laxity and
of reducing to an artificial formality the whole scheme of

penitence and restoration to grace. This came about in three
stages. There was, first, a strong reaction in the Celtic church
against the life-long disabilities of the old system of public
penance, and against long periods of excommunication. In
itself, this reaction was right, but it was open to being mis-
understood as evidence of a less serious estimation of the
gravity of sin. Nevertheless, the penances imposed at this
stage were still severe, and were often of many years' dura-
tion. They might include exile, imprisonment, pilgrimages
and fines as well as impositions of prayer and fasting. And the
fasting was not light, e.g. seven years on bread and water, or
"special fasts" of complete abstinence from all food for two
whole days and a night, repeated at intervals during a year.
During this first stage, it became the custom to admit the
penitent to communion after eighteen months even though
he had not yet completed the performance of the penance
imposed upon him. Consequently, there was an inevitable
tendency to shorten the penance itself, so that it should not
outlast the period of the excommunication. This ended in
the second stage in which the "composition" or "commuta-
tion" of penance has become the usual thing.

The Old Irish Table of Commutations (eighth century)
contains a whole series of such compositions, whereby the
length of a period of penance might be shortened by the
performance of ascetic exercises. In this way the usual long
penances of fasting, with all their attendant inconveniences
to the penitent and his household, could be avoided. The
compositions were sometimes eccentric and sometimes extremely exacting. We read of sleeping in water, in nettles, on
nut-shells, or with a dead body in a grave. (The Old Irish
Table of Commutations 8, p. 144.) Or in the same table we
are told that a composition for a week of hard penance on
bread and water is "seven Beati" (i.e. Psalm 119 seven times
—7 x 176 verses) in honest cross-vigil (i.e. standing with arms
extended like a cross) and a credo and paternoster and
hymnum dicat with every beatitude (No. 26). It is difficult
to believe that such penances could do much to induce

penitence, or to build up a love of righteousness. Rather, they clearly assume the character of punishment, pure and simple. The underlying idea would seem to be that certain actions have to be paid for, either in this life or the next. But once they are paid for, they become a part of the past and are of no further importance. The prime consideration is not the awakening of contrition, nor the imploring of God's un-merited forgiveness in union with the perfect self-offering of Christ on Calvary, but the payment of the satisfaction which crimes demand. The emphasis seems to fall far too heavily on what *we* must do to atone for our sins in this life if we are to escape the pains of hell; and there is far too little said about a change of heart or of the Cross as our only means of Atonement. For example, consider the first and second clauses of the Old Irish Table of Commutations (p. 142):

1. "The composition for saving a soul out of hell, viz. 365 paternosters and 365 genuflexions and 365 blows with a scourge on every day to the end of a year, and fasting every month saves a soul out of hell. For this composition for re-deeming the soul that deserves torments in the body has been made according to the number of joints and sinews that are in a man's body."

2. "Another composition, viz. the three fifties every day, with their conclusion of the Beati to the end of seven years, saves a soul out of hell."

The explanation of this strongly-marked externalism and formalism lies partly, perhaps, in a misunderstanding of the writings of the Fathers about penance. The Fathers constantly speak of penance as a medicine and describe the works en-joined by penance—prayer, fasting and almsgiving—as a long medical treatment whereby the patient is slowly cured of the evil results and vicious habits of his sinful nature, and of that sinfulness as well. In the thought of the Fathers it is quite clear that this long healing process is throughout con-ditional on the enabling power of the divine grace, and pre-supposes a prior act of divine forgiveness. One of their favourite texts for a penitential sermon was the raising of

Lazarus. Christ calls Lazarus to life—"Come forth". This is the operation of the divine grace awakening the sinner to repentance and creating within him a contrite heart. The disciples loose him, i.e. the Church, by the medicine of the penance, frees him from the clogging bands of sin. But it was not difficult for this teaching to come to be understood as laying chief stress on the penitential works as themselves being the means of procuring forgiveness, or rather of making satisfaction for sins. A further explanation of the character of the teaching in the Penitentials may lie in the general Pelagian bias of the Celtic and Anglo-Saxon peoples.

It is not altogether surprising to find that in the later Penitentials a further third step has been taken. Not only can the longer period of penance be shortened by the performance of concentrated ascetic exercises and the "prayer-wheel" recitations of Psalter and Paternosters, but this satisfaction can now be rendered by someone else on the sinner's behalf. After all, what matters, it seems, is that the penance be done, the satisfaction be made. If a rich man can order or bribe someone else to do it for him, what matter, so long as it be done? Consider this extract from the tenth-century "Canons of King Edgar" (p. 410):

"Thus may a powerful man and rich in friends with the support of his friends greatly lighten his penance: After confession let him undertake penance with much sighing, lay aside his weapons and wear woolen or hair cloth garments and so do, that in three days the series of vii years be dispensed with thus; let him proceed with aid; and first let him take with him xii men, and let them fast iii days on bread, and on green herbs, and on water; and get, in addition thereto, in whatever manner he can, seven times cxx men, who shall also fast for him iii days; then will be fasted as many fasts as there are days in vii years."

This document contains, also, numerous examples of the commuting of penance into gifts, whereby a rich man is caused the minimum of inconvenience.

When, therefore, we consider how these penitentials
c

contradict certain important provisions of the old law, when we note the wide variety of the penances demanded for the same sin, when we observe their chaotic individualism and their ever-increasing laxity, it is not to be wondered at that the Carolingian reformers sought by every means in their power to suppress them. Council after council forbade their use. But it was a hopeless cause. The Penitentials had come to stay. Parts of them found their way into the body of the Canon Law. Their underlying idea permeated it.

The idea, I mean, that it is a proper part of the canon law to provide machinery for punishing the sins of clergy and laity and for coercing them into respectability if not righteousness. This idea had little, if any, place in the old law. The old law had, it is true, provisions for the disciplining of clergy and laity, but these were chiefly aimed at securing that the public teaching of the Church was not compromised by the apparent condonation of grave sin—it was for this reason that persons guilty of particular conduct were prevented from being ordained or were excommunicated. These provisions were not aimed directly at the punishment and coercion of sinners. By reason of the Penitentials canon law became assimilated with secular law in the sense that it began to concern itself directly with a penal discipline. Not content with laying down a minimum standard of conduct consistent with membership of the Church, it proceeded to establish a system of punishing offenders for their sins, whilst retaining them within the Christian fellowship. It became, in fact, a sort of handmaid or assistant to the secular law in its work of maintaining order and regulating morals. And for this end, it employed alike temporal and spiritual sanctions, to the extreme detriment of the true nature and purpose of the latter.

But we must return to our more immediate subject. The Carolingian reform failed in both its objects. It did not suppress the Penitentials. That was, indeed, a hopeless task. They were too useful as rough and ready guides to the clergy in their pastoral work, and they enjoyed, in consequence, an

immense popularity. In the end, the reformers bowed to the
storm, and were content to produce Penitentials of their own
which should be more in conformity with the old law which
they were trying to re-establish. But not even in this were
they successful. For the old Penitentials remained in use, and
others like them continued to be produced.

The reformers failed in their other object also, that of reforming the Church as a whole; or at least, they failed to
achieve all that they set out to effect. Their initial successes in
the realm of the morals and manners of the clergy and laity
were ultimately jeopardised by their failure in respect of
ecclesiastical property. The support of the Crown in the rest of
their reforms was bought at the price of the complete subjection of the temporalities of the Church to royal domination.
Charlemagne and his successors evicted, it is true, aristo-
cratic lay encroachers on Church property: but they reserved
in their own hands the patronage of what they had saved.
They put in, as bishops, their own nominees, and made of
them their vassals. Sometimes they kept a bishopric empty
for a long period, and administered its estates through laymen, to their own profit. They taxed heavily those clerics
whom they placed in office. Sometimes, in order to get pos-
session of the revenues of a bishopric, they would cause him
to be accused of some crime, judge the case themselves, and
evict him. The bishops were helpless against a secular power
determined to ignore the ecclesiastical law or to re-make it
in their own interests. The hierarchy was brought into complete dependence on the civil powers, and the spiritual
quality of its members in consequence declined. Whenever
a bishop arose with sufficient courage to attempt to recover
independence by re-establishing ecclesiastical rights of patronage and freehold, he was promptly accused of cupidity and
avarice. It was in vain for him to plead the old law and the
rights of the Church, or to point to the Scriptural command-
ments to pay tithes and oblations. He met the same hostile
reply: that he was seeking only to feather his own nest. And
the reply was the more difficult to counter because the laws

and texts on which the bishop had to rely were not such as bore any immediate and obvious application or relevance to the case in hand. Indeed, how could they? For they were framed within a civilisation—the Roman Empire—which had passed away, and with a view to meeting totally different situations. And very often they were couched in purely general terms.

And so a new method had to be tried. It was simple but audacious. Since the secular authorities would not grant the reforms desired, the reforms should be represented as having been granted long ago by earlier kings and laws. The laws which could not be passed now, should be forged and set forth as old law newly discovered. They might be secular laws passed by kings or spiritual laws enacted by the Church; better still, they might be both. In this way were born the False Capitularies and the False Decretals. The False Capitularies either claim the authority of the Emperor, or of the Pope or a council in conjunction with the Emperor. They are for the most part made up of extracts from genuine councils. Sometimes they are taken from Dionysius or the Hispana: very often they come from the reforming councils held in the time of Charlemagne, often from the letters of popes. But wherever they come from, they are represented, with suitable alterations and additions to the text, as having been expressly assented to by one of the bygone emperors; "according to the canons of the Holy Fathers and the edicts of the emperors" is the kind of description given to the provisions of these collections. The forgeries are, on the whole, skilful. There are occasional lapses when the author, forgetting that he is attributing to the Emperor some extract from a papal letter, leaves in a reference to "our brother bishops". But in general care is taken to ensure plausibility. Texts are inserted dealing with other matters than those which are the chief preoccupation of the authors, lest a continual harping on one or two themes should arouse suspicions too violently. So, these False Capitularies contain

much which is strictly relevant to secular law as well as purely ecclesiastical matter.

The False Decretals claim to be authentic Papal letters which the author has been at pains to collect and assemble, and which he publishes, by request, to satisfy an urgent need for accurate knowledge of the ancient canons. The author is said to be one Isidorus Mercator, and his collection falls into three parts. The first contains some introductory matter and then a long series of wholly false decretals attributed to a succession of popes from Clement I to Melchiades (310–14). The second part consists mainly of canons, taken from the Hispana; that is, of the Greek and African Councils, together with those of the Gallican councils down to II Arles, and of the Spanish councils down to XIII Toledo. These are all genuine texts, though in places there are interpolations. There is a certain amount of prefatory material, including the famous "Donation of Constantine" in which Constantine is alleged at his conversion to have richly endowed the Church with lands and privileges. This is an entirely false document, of course, but it is not the work of Isidore. He may even have believed it to be genuine. The third part corresponds to the second part of the Hispana and consists of the decretals of Popes from Sylvester (314) to Gregory II (721). They are genuine decretals, but in places adapted, to which have been added more than thirty forged decretals.

The forgeries throughout are cleverly done. Many of the False Decretals are made to concern matters of theology and other points quite irrelevant to the chief interests of the forgers. In this way an increased air of verisimilitude is given to the collection. The decretals are formed—it must have been an immense labour involving a profound knowledge of the genuine papal letters—of a mosaic of sentences and phrases taken from authentic Roman documents and strung together in such a way as to give the required sense. Their place of origin is now thought to be the Province of Tours. It is quite certain that they were *not* fabricated in Rome.

Throughout France they had an immediate success, and they provide material for many subsequent canonical collections; indeed they may be said almost to dominate the canonical literature of the Middle Ages. They were not, however, accepted at Rome, or used by the Popes until the Gregorian reforms of the eleventh century. From then on they are universally accepted and figure in all the collections, including that of Gratian, as being of equal authority and value with the ancient canons. It was not until the fifteenth century that their authenticity was questioned: they were finally demonstrated to be false by the Calvinist, Blondel, in 1628. Blondel's arguments were accepted by the Church of Rome.

The fundamental ideas which underlie this tremendous enterprise in forgery are clear. In the first place it was to safeguard ecclesiastical property. To this end texts are found or forged stating that all the temporal possessions of the Church are sacrosanct, consecrated to God for ever, which it is sacrilege to put to secular uses or to alienate into secular hands. Secondly, the intention of the forgers was to free the clergy from the performance of secular duties, particularly from the obligation to render military service to which they had become subjected by reason of their dependance on the great nobles. Thirdly, it was their aim to protect the clergy from the secular power and avarice. They set out prominently all the old laws governing the trial and accusations of bishops —there were plenty to their hand in the classical tradition; that bishops are to be tried only by their brother bishops, that their accusers must be persons of good standing in the Church, and so on. And they extended, where necessary, the application of these laws to the inferior clergy as well. In other words the system of "benefit of clergy", that the clergy are to be tried only in the spiritual courts is worked out in detail. Fourthly, they sought to protect the French Church as a whole from falling a prey to the powerful laity. To this end, they stressed the sovereign power of the Pope. For in the light of past experience, they believed that in the central authority of the

papacy lay the one hope of preserving a local church from being dominated by the local nobility. Therefore, they insisted that the old law provided for everyone a right of appeal to Rome, and that the final decision of every dispute lies in the hands of the Pope. Particularly they insisted that all cases involving a bishop were expressly reserved to the Pope and that no bishop could be deposed except by him. By the same emphasis on the Papal power they sought also to remove the canon law itself from any danger of being corrupted by the influence of the local nobility. They adduced laws to show that the Pope is supreme over councils, and that no conciliar decisions are valid or operative until they have been ratified by him.

In addition to these measures designed to save the Church from outside interference, the creators of these forged collections sought to reform the Church within. Here they pinned their hopes on the Diocesan bishop. They carefully stressed the old territorial organisation of the Church centred round the city and diocese—so unlike the Celtic system with its monastic bishops and wandering bishops, men with no real authority and little more than ordaining agents: a system calculated to introduce and foster anarchy and disorder. Thus these reformers were particularly hostile in their writings to the "chorepiscopi", assistant bishops, men of mediocre quality, who were at that time numerous in France and by means of whom the Diocesan bishops found the leisure necessary for the discharge of their many secular duties. At the same time they subordinated the parochial clergy strictly to the authority of the Diocesan, in accordance with the ancient tradition. And they subjected the monasteries, too, to his control. Indeed the Diocesan bishop emerges clearly in these writings as the central pillar of Church Order. Within his diocese he is supreme: his authority cannot be shared with others nor delegated. The clergy are little more than his curates: the monasteries are under his supervision.

With the same intention of exalting the authority of the Bishop, the powers of metropolitans are diminished. The

province is not governed by the personal authority of the
Archbishop; it is governed by the synod of the diocesan
bishops, of which the Archbishop is merely the president.
For this, of course, they found ample authority in the Greek
councils, especially in the council of Antioch. Above the
Metropolitan is placed the Primate or Patriarch. His position
and functions are left very ill defined. Indeed it is not easy
to see where he fits in, especially in view of the exalted position accorded to the Pope.

Having thus sought to re-establish the independence and
order of the Church, the Reformers recalled the clergy to
their duty of loyal obedience to the old canonical rules of
conduct both in public worship and in the ordering of their
private lives. Similarly they recalled the laity to the standards
of Christian morality, especially in the matter of marriage.
Thus in one way and another the Pseudo-Isidorian collections cover the whole sphere of canon law.

The influence of these writings upon the development of
canon law is, without any doubt, enormous. The authority
of the Pope owes much to them. It is not true that they created
the idea of the Papal supremacy; they found it in existence
and used it as a means of protecting the French Church from
secular interference. But they gave to the idea a sharper
clarity and precision, and were instrumental in popularising
it. Again, all those large sections of the later canon law which
are devoted to the removal of the trial of bishops and clergy
from the secular courts to the spiritual are profoundly in-
fluenced by these writings. Also, to them is largely due the
whole conception of the sacro-sanctity of Church property.
But perhaps their most striking influence is to be found in
the matter of the authority of the bishop. Here they seem both
to have reproduced the old law and to have profoundly
modified it. In stressing the authority of the bishop within
his own diocese, and of the synod in the province they were
reproducing the old law. In subordinating the clergy so
strictly, and in making the bishop a lone and autocratic
figure, they were innovating. There is, I think, room for a

close study of the effect of the Pseudo-Isidorian collections
on the doctrine of episcopacy.

A similar study might well be made of the rights and duties,
privileges and powers of an Archbishop. For example, in
the case of the Archbishop of Canterbury it is well known
that some of his powers are derived not from his Archbishopric as such, but from an inheritance at the Reformation of
certain Papal powers. Other of his privileges derive from his
pre-Reformation status of Papal legate. Others again from
his office of Primate. Yet it is by no means always clear
which power comes from which source. It would, in my
judgement, be of great value to trace the development of the
Archbishopric of Canterbury with a view to showing what
is essential and what is accidental to the office of an archbishop, and to demonstrating how and in what degree the
original relationship of the Metropolitan to his Suffragans,
as it is contained in the classical canon law, has been modified or transformed by the impact of the doctrine of the
Papal Supremacy. And in any such studies the writings
which we have just been considering would prove, I think,
to be of vital importance.

THE CREATION OF THE CORPUS

THE reforms attempted by the False Capitularies and Decretals were only partially successful. The example set of interpolation, adaptation and forgery proved infectious and was quickly followed by others. All canonists felt themselves at liberty to interpret their sources as they wished and in accordance with local custom or temporary needs. Thus the next period is one of growing confusion and diversity. It was followed, at the beginning of the eleventh century by a new reforming movement begun under the leadership of the Emperor Henry II. It is reflected, in the history of canon law, by the important collection known as the "Decretum of Burchard of Worms". Burchard was a kind of prince-bishop. For the town of Worms was not only his diocese: it lay under his temporal authority as well. A great deal of his time and effort was devoted to the reorganisation and reform of the town's civic life and to a codification of its laws.

Somewhere between 1008 and 1012 Burchard undertook a similar work of reform and codification on behalf of the Church and for the guidance of his brother bishops. He compiled a complete collection of the canon law. He divided the work into twenty books, of which these are the subject matter. (1) Papacy, metropolitans, bishops, councils, appeals, etc. (2) The lower clergy. (3) Church buildings, tithes, fees, etc. (4) Baptism, and Confirmation. (5) Eucharist. (6) Murder. (7) Incest. (8) Monks and nuns. (9) Virgins, rape: marriage. (10) Magic and sorcery. (11) Excommunications: theft and robbery. (12) Perjury. (13) Fasting. (14) Gluttony and drunkenness. (15) Emperors, princes and other laity. (16) Procedure in the Spiritual Courts. (17) Fornication and other forms of immorality. (18) Visitation and absolution of the

sick. (19) A Penitential: known as the Corrector and often published separately later. (20) Theological matters.

Burchard's main sources were the Hadriana and the False Decretals. These he either quotes directly, or through the medium of two later collections which were based on them.[1] For the penitential book he drew on the stock penitentials, with a certain preference for those of the ninth century of German origin. It is true that he professes to limit himself to three of the Penitentials, but in this he is not being honest. Indeed in the whole matter of the use and description of his sources he shows himself the son of his age, and assumes a freedom and latitude which can only be described as shocking, if one looks at it from the point of view of the modern historian and scholar. But then, of course, there are other points of view. Certainly Burchard was more concerned with making his texts effective than with describing or transcribing them accurately. Thus he rarely, if ever, allows it to be seen that any of his texts are those of secular edicts or laws. He prefers, if that is the case, either to give no indication of their source, or quite simply to ascribe them to a Pope, an early council or to one of the Fathers—particularly to St. Augustine. Nor did this freedom of treatment stop at the ascription of the material: he altered and adapted the text of his sources to give the meaning which he required. And if that proved impossible, he would forge a new canon and attribute it to some genuine council, or if necessary invent canon and council alike. In all this he conceived himself to be acting in the interests of truth, order and justice.

It will be worth while to spend a little time on this collection and its author, because by means of this collection much new matter entered into the canon law, and the whole work is an instructive example of the adaptation and development of the old law to meet the demands of a new and more complicated situation.

Burchard himself seems to have been, by nature, a man of

[1] Those known as the "Collection of Reginon of Prum" and the "Anselmo Dedicata".

moderate views, a compromiser. Thus, whilst stoutly up-
holding the role of the temporal power as guardian of the
Church, the restorer of order and the enforcer of canonical
rules, he is careful, as we have seen, not to allow to it the role
of ecclesiastical legislator. It is the same with the Papacy.
He has no doubts whatever about the supreme position of
the Bishop of Rome. The Pope is the head, and he is charged
with authority as law-giver, ruler and judge. Burchard
knows of no better way of investing a rule with authority
than by ascribing it to one of the Popes. Yet where other
collections expatiate on the rights and the powers of the
Roman Church, Burchard is almost silent. It is the middle
way: the Pope is supreme, but we must not exaggerate. This
position is illustrated by his attitude to two burning questions
of the day:

1. *Monastic exemptions.* Strong supporters of the Papacy were
at this time advocating the subjection of monasteries immediately to the Pope and their withdrawal from the jurisdiction of the Diocesan Bishop. In support of this thesis there
were some well known canonical texts. Burchard omits these
texts and is silent on the whole matter. On the other hand, he
is careful to insert and adapt texts in order to stress the right
of a bishop to visit and inspect monasteries in his diocese.

2. *Pilgrimages to Rome.* The practice was increasing whereby
lay-people, when guilty of grave sin, were going straight to
Rome in the hope of getting absolution on easier terms there
than they would at home. Burchard approves of a pilgrimage
to Rome as a pious spiritual exercise, but insists that before
setting off penitents must first confess their sins at home, because it is their own bishop who has over them authority to
bind and loose. He maintains also that such a pilgrimage
does not absolve the penitent from the necessity of perform-
ing the penance which has been laid upon him.

Indeed, as in the False Decretals, so in Burchard's Decretum, it is the authority of the bishop which holds the
central place. Within his diocese he is supreme, and he
represents his diocese in the councils of the Church. Burchard

lays emphasis, too, on the provisions of the old law against the translation of bishops. In theory at least, the bishop is wedded to his diocese for life, and may not leave it for another and more important See. In theory; but in practice Burchard recognised the necessity and advantage of the existing custom which permitted a bishop to be translated where the advantage of the Church evidently demanded it. A bishop could not, of course, be deposed by the secular power but only by his ecclesiastical superiors. And those superiors are not the Metropolitan alone. The trial and deposition of a bishop is a matter for the provincial synod, over which the Metropolitan presides; but only presides. He is not the synod itself. The bishop has, of course, a right of appeal from the synod to Rome. But in general Burchard regards the Pope as a distant authority only intervening on rare occasions and in matters of exceptional importance. The normal authority is the bishop, with his provincial synod in immediate superiority over him.

The compromising, practical working of Burchard's mind is shown in his treatment of the pressing problem raised by the law requiring the celibacy of the clergy. At this time in many parts of Europe including Germany, it had become almost the regular thing for the secular, parochial clergy to marry. They could not marry in law, but they could and did marry in fact and brought up families of children all of whom, because there could be no legal marriage, were illegitimate. This in itself was a further and serious problem for ecclesiastical authority. Burchard firmly re-asserted the old law which, by numerous canons, forbade the clergy to marry. But having stated the principle, he then faced the facts. He did not do what his successors were to do a generation or so later—forbid the faithful to receive the Sacraments from the hands of a married priest. He did the opposite: he inserted a canon of Gangra (4) which explicitly condemns those who refuse to take the Sacrament from a priest on the sole ground that he is married.

With regard to the clergy, Burchard strove hard to correct

the then prevalent corruptions of avarice and simony. Pluralism was rife and the clergy treated their benefices merely as so many sources of income. They so administered their endowments, and so avidly extracted gifts and dues from the laity that they amassed for themselves considerable private fortunes. So considerable, that many were found anxious to buy their own way into such profitable offices. Burchard reproduces a host of texts to condemn simony in every shape and form: he condemned also the practice of charging fees for ministerial services. Surplice fees—fees, that is, for conducting burials, celebrating weddings and such like—he regarded with abhorrence. It was not till later that the canon law clearly distinguished between the celebration of the Sacraments, the charging of a fee for which is simony, and other services for which an offering may be solicited or demanded from the laity. Simony, fees, offerings, dues, occupy a not insignificant section of the canon law: it is with Burchard that they begin to come into that prominence. And the same is true of pluralities. Burchard condemns them outright. The later canon law will contain many provisions for their strict regulation and control.

Another problem confronted Burchard in the relation of the local nobility to the churches which they had themselves built on their own estates. There was little law as yet directly bearing on this point. The church so built was the private property of the builder, who could transfer it to whom he liked. The appointment of a priest to minister in it was entirely in his hands, and so was his dismissal. The priest was as much subject to his Lord's pleasures and whims in the church as the miller was in the mill or a farmer in his farm. The authority of the bishop counted for little or nothing. Burchard inserts into his Decretum a number of texts designed to limit these powers of the local magistrates and to free the priest from his state of complete subjection. Thus he lays it down that no church shall be founded without the consent of the Bishop, and that that consent will not be given unless there is an adequate endowment. No one may

be appointed to a church unless first approved by the Bishop. Once appointed, he cannot be dismissed by the patron without the consent of the Bishop. Here we see, in an early stage of its development, that large section of the canon law devoted to institution, and to the "parsons freehold".

The Decretum, and especially the Corrector or Penitential within it, contains numerous rules concerning the morals of the laity and attempts to soften and civilise the brutal manners of the age. The indissolubility of marriage is strongly asserted, though under the influence of the Penitentials one or two exceptions are allowed. There is an attempt to restrain blood feuds, to condemn perjury, to stamp out magic and to check drunkenness. In all this Burchard follows the Penitentials and borrows largely from them. He does it in the spirit of the Penitentials at their best: that is, he exhorts the confessor to examine carefully each penitent and to weigh the circumstances of each sin. He is to treat every sinner and every sin on their own merits and not blindly to apply a rule of thumb. The role of moral theology in canon law takes another step forward.

The influence of this great collection cannot be exaggerated. It becomes a source of all later works, down to and including Gratian. No doubt this immediate popularity and lasting influence was due in part to its compromising nature. It was essentially a practical, and therefore a useful book. Its popularity, however, did not extend south of the Alps. In Italy and Rome it found little favour. Its marked reserve in the matter of the Papacy and its use of the Penitentials would combine to make the work unpalatable there. All the more so when, in the latter half of the century the reforms connected with the name of Pope Gregory VII or Hildebrand began to make their influence felt.

These Gregorian reforms were concerned, first and foremost with the consolidation and enhancement of the position of the Pope as supreme head of the Church and Vicar of Christ. Secondly they dealt with what had become the most pressing contemporary problem in which the issue of the

Papal supremacy was deeply involved. This was the superiority of the spiritual over the temporal power; and the battle
was fought out over the question of lay investiture. Who gave
the clergy, and especially the bishops, their authority?
Emperor or Pope, Church or State?

Thirdly, they dealt with the validity of heretical Sacraments. At that date this issue centred round the Sacraments
and especially Ordination administered by persons guilty of
simony. And fourthly they dealt with the question of the
legitimacy of the use of force in defence of the Church. These
reforms produced several collections of authentic canons and
decretals and included with them extracts from the old
Roman civil law of Justinian. It is thus that the civil law came
to play so large a part in the canon law. They also inspired,
though they did not dominate, the next great collection to
form a milestone in the development of the Western canon
law—the Decretum of Ivo.

Ivo was Bishop of Chartres and his great canonical work
dates from about 1094. The main source is Burchard, and
one of the Gregorian collections known as the Britannica.
To these are added many texts from the Roman civil law
(Justinian), and a number of important excerpts from the
Fathers on theological matters. The main tendency of the
collection is in line with the Gregorian Reform. It stresses
the Papal supremacy. But it exhibits the same practical
compromising spirit as Burchard. Thus although clearly up-
holding the doctrine of the supreme legislative power of the
Pope—the *plenitudo potestatis*—Ivo regards with disfavour and
attempts to check the newly developing custom by which the
Pope sought to entrust the exercise of that power to delegates
in the form of *legati nati*; that is, to the system of attributing
a general superior jurisdiction to the holders of important
primatial Sees. In particular Ivo opposed the growing claims
of this nature put forward by the Archbishop of Lyons. Similarly in the matter of lay investiture, Ivo is quite clear on the
principle that the spiritual power is superior to the temporal:
but he deprecates an out and out clash between Church and

State and is ready to support a compromise which recognises to the temporal power a right to invest a duly appointed and duly consecrated bishop with the insignia of a purely temporal rank and jurisdiction: provided that it be made clear that such a lay investiture carries with it no spiritual significance at all. Though this was not an acceptable solution to his contemporaries, in the next generation it triumphed. In the case of English bishops, it still obtains.

Perhaps Ivo's greatest contribution to the development of the canon law, however, was not this Decretum— a large work in 17 books made up of 3,760 items—nor his other two great canonical writings (Panormia: Tripartitum) but is contained in the Prologue to the Decretum. For here he lays down certain rules and principles for the interpretation and harmonising of texts, which have had an incalculable effect upon the whole system of canonical jurisprudence. All canonists of this period were confronted with a number of conflicting rulings on almost every subject. Ivo advises them how to proceed to unravel the contradictions or to arrive at a decision on which of the conflicting rules is to be obeyed. First of all, he says, a text must be placed against its historical background and examined in relation to its context in order that its true meaning and bearing may become plain. Secondly, texts must be carefully scrutinised and their ascription tested, so that forgeries may be eliminated. Thirdly, one must observe a certain hierarchy of authority, and where two texts conflict, that one must be obeyed which emanates from the higher authority—a canon from a general council takes precedence over one from a local provincial council; a text from a Papal letter over-rides a provision of a general council. Fourthly, and of cardinal importance—I shall return to it in my last lecture—a distinction must be made between laws which are variable and those which are invariable. When this is done many an apparent contradiction may be seen to be due to a dispensation in a special case from a general variable law. Both contradictory rules are true, but one is general and the other particular.

D

In all this Ivo was wholly in accord with his contemporary Bernold of Constance, and together they paved the way for the great harmonising work of Gratian in the next generation. With Gratian we arrive at the first part of the final and fully constituted Corpus Juris Canonici, the Law Book of the late Middle Ages, and of the Church of Rome until its official revision and conversion into the Codex Juris Canonici in 1917.

When Gratian compiled his Decretum in 1140 he was faced, like his predecessors, with a multiplicity of conflicting texts. The position in this respect had been greatly worsened by the intrusion of various theological issues into canon law in the course of the controversy over Berengarius and transubstantiation, and in the efforts to stamp out simony and heresies. In these various disputes each side fortified itself with canonical and patristic texts, which passed impartially into the canonical collections and so made them full of contradictions. It was the great work of Gratian to attempt to harmonise them.

Gratian collected from the earlier works, especially from Ivo and from the False Decretals, a total of 3,458 texts. They come from the Bible, from Councils, from the writings of the Fathers, from Papal letters, from the civil law, from the Penitentials. They comprise all of church law that Gratian thought important and worth preserving. Scarcely anything of value in the earlier collections has been omitted. They are arranged into three parts. The first consists of 101 Distinctions—sub-divided into Canons—the first 20 deal with the sources of the canon law, the remainder with the hierarchy. The second part is divided into 36 Causes. Each Cause raises a series of Questions, and each Question is dealt with separately and at length in a number of canons. The general method—and it is similar to that followed in the first part—is to give a series of texts which favour the answer "no" (or "yes") to the particular question, followed by another series favouring the opposite or a qualified and different answer. Then Gratian suggests a distinction which ought to be made

and finally proposes his own solution with another series of texts to support it. There is therefore interspersed among the texts cited a sort of running commentary; and in order to determine what was Gratian's opinion on any point of law, it is never enough merely to find some particular canon in his Decretum. It is necessary to look at the canons which precede and follow it and to read Gratian's own dicta, by reference to which alone is it possible to see whether this particular canon is part of the series which he favours or of one which he is later going to counter.

In the last of the 36 Causes Gratian raises as Question No. 3 the subject of Penance, and this, not surprisingly, involves him in what is virtually a separate thesis. Here he reverts to the division of his material into Distinctions and canons as in the first part of his work. To avoid confusion, when this part is quoted the words De Paenitentia are added to the number of the Distinction and canon. The third part of the work is devoted to a treatment of Churches and Sacraments and Public Worship generally. It, too, is divided into Distinctions and canons and is referred to as the De Consecratione.

This superb adaptation of the Scholastic Method in Theology to the treatment of canon law—no one with the slightest familiarity with the writings of the Schoolmen can fail to be reminded, on glancing at Gratian, of the "sic et non", or of the "videtur quod; sed contra: respondeo dicendum" of Aquinas—marked a tremendous advance in juridical method. The texts are dated and put in their historical setting; they are illumined by explanations and commentaries; the final solutions are amply supported by further legal evidence. Canon Law has become a science. The success was immediate and lasting. The book superseded all earlier collections, and became *the* book of the canon law, a text book in constant use for centuries. There is a certain irony in this. Gratian's work contributed perhaps more than any other single influence to the final establishment throughout Western Europe of the theory of the absolute Papal

supremacy. For in Gratian's work it is made abundantly
clear that it is the Pope's authority which gives validity to
all Church law and that it is from the Pope, and the Pope
alone, that any fresh universally binding law can come, and
that no local church law can stand against the Pope's dis-
sent. The Pope is the fount of Law. It was on this foundation,
so clearly and finally laid by Gratian, that the succeeding
Popes built. Yet Gratian's work itself never received official
authorisation in Rome. It was a private work. Consequently,
in theory, no text had any juridical force simply because it
was in Gratian: it had only whatever juridical force belonged
to it in itself. Neither were Gratian's own dicta authoritative
in themselves. All the same, in fact, the work was accorded all
the respect and careful study which belong to an officially
promulgated document. It was a part of the Corpus, and
whatever the theory may be, was in fact a part of "the law",
subject to later interpretation and to the decrees of later
Popes.

Both interpretation and decrees quickly followed. The
former came in the shape of the comments and glosses of the
series of great canon lawyers who succeeded Gratian and
who, because they were writing on or about the Decretum,
are known as the Decretists. The last of these, Johannes
Teutonicus, wrote what is called the Glossa Ordinaria—the
series of notes, explanations and references printed in the
margins of the ordinary editions of the Corpus. The latter
came in the numerous Decretals of the immediately succeeding Popes.

The date of the issue of Gratian's Decretum was followed
by the reigns of a number of active, energetic and legally
expert Popes—e.g. Innocent III and Alexander III. These
Popes quickly took advantage of the clear sharp conception
of the Papal supremacy made current by Gratian and em-
barked on a course of intense legislative activity. It was not
long, therefore, before there was in existence a substantial
body of law to which the Decretum made no reference. This
was a manifest inconvenience. In Gratian's Decretum there

was indeed a first-class legal textbook but it did not include
the many new additions to the law contained in recent
Papal decrees. With every year which passed, Gratian grew
out of date, or rather incomplete. Accordingly a number of
unofficial collections of the latest Decretals were made, to
meet this defect. In 1234, almost a century after the first
publication of the Decretum these unofficial collections were
superseded by the official publication, under a Bull of
Gregory IX, of the Collection known as "The Extravagants
of Gregory IX". Extravagant, because extra vagantes,
wandering outside the Decretum of Gratian. The matter of
this collection consists of 1971 items divided into five books,
each of which is sub-divided into titles and chapters. The
general subject matter of each book is as follows. Book I,
Sources of Law, the grades of the hierarchy and the jurisdiction belonging to each grade. Book II, Procedure in the
Spiritual Courts. Book III, The rights and duties of the
Clergy and of religious communities. Book IV, Marriage.
Book V, Moral offences and their treatment and punishment,
with an appendix on legal rules and aphorisms.

In 1298 Boniface VIII authorised the publication of a
further collection, of the decretals issued after the reign of
Gregory IX. This collection also is divided into five books
and the titles are the same as those in the Extravagants. This
collection is known as the Sext—the sixth book after the five
of Pope Gregory's collection. In 1314 Clement V published
the Clementine Constitutions, with the same arrangement
in five books as the two earlier collections.

The Bulls which authorised the issue of the Extravagants
and the Sext stated that no Papal decree outside these collections had legal validity and that no collections of such
decrees were to be made. The Bull which accompanied the
Clementine Constitutions contained no such provision. Consequently for this later period private collections of decretals
were made. Two of them found their way into the final form
of the Corpus—namely the Extravagants of John XXII,
containing 20 constitutions of that Pope, and the Extra-

vagantes Communes, a series of 70 decretals of various Popes between 1294 and 1484.

We have reached the end of the creative period. The law of Western Christendom in the Middle Ages is now complete. It is to be found in the Corpus Juris Canonici published by Jean Chapuis in 1503. This consists of Gratian, of the three officially published collections of Decretals and of these last two private collections just mentioned. With Chapuis' work the code of canon law as a code is closed and fixed until its revision in 1917. The development of the legal system of the Roman Church henceforth consisted in the addition to the Code of the decisions of the various Holy Offices through which the Pope exercises his legislative, administrative and interpretative powers. But the Code itself remained unchanged. It was, supremely, the law: the wonder, delight and admiration of the canonists of the later Middle Ages: a system complex but well-nigh complete. Its use, in the courts, required deep learning and a retentive memory. It is extraordinarily hard to track down any particular text to its hiding-place among these cumbrous pages. And that text, when found, must be supplemented by, contrasted with or reconciled with many other texts lurking elsewhere in the Corpus. To facilitate this was the purpose and work of the Glossators, who soon did for the Decretals what their predecessors had done for the Decretum—filled the margin with learned notes, interpretations and cross-references.

This completed Corpus Juris Canonici was the law in force at the time of the Reformation. As to the old law—as the Canonists called Gratian's Decretum, in distinction from the "new law" of the Decretal Collections—it was drawn, as we have seen, from a multitude of sources. The new law has but one source—the Pope. Yet the whole is made to rest on the sovereign Papal power. It is from the Pope that it derives its authority; he alone has full right to alter it, interpret it, or to allow exceptions to its general provisions. It is this factor which created such complications for Henry VIII when he threw off the Papal yoke at the Reformation, and it is to this

factor, in consequence, that the importance of the Statute law in the Church of England is largely due. But of that I shall have something to say in the next lecture.

This canon law was administered wholly in the spiritual courts by spiritual persons. It lay outside the sphere of the temporal courts and their lay judges. It was an international or supra-national legal system, developed and existing independently of and alongside the national or King's law, from which it differed both in content and in the method of its administration. For the canon law contained more of the old Roman law—especially in the form of rules of interpretation and procedure—and less of local Germanic, Frankish or Anglo-Saxon law than did the civil codes. To this canon law all Christian people were subject, clergy and laity alike, and there were few activities and departments of life to which it was not relevant.

What was the relation of England to this canon law? Down to the Norman Conquest, the English Church had for law its indigenous penitentials. These were largely based on local custom, but contained also—perhaps through the Oriental Archbishop Theodore, to whom are ascribed, falsely, a great number of penitentials—canons of Greek councils, extracts from the Fathers, Eastern and Western, and many biblical texts. To these must be added the decisions of Anglo-Saxon Councils. There was plenty of law, but it was greatly confused. William the Conqueror set about restoring order. He brought in as Archbishop of Canterbury the Norman-bred Lanfranc. Lanfranc's first task was to give to the English Church a code. We have it now, surviving in a number of manuscripts in England. It consisted of large extracts from the False Decretals. That is to say, one series of the Hispana canons, and one series of Decretals from Clement to Gregory II. To these is to be added another little work belonging to the Pseudo-Isidorian Collections, known as the Capitula Angilrami, which establishes spiritual jurisdiction over the clergy, and withdraws them from the civil courts. Many manuscripts of this collection, of a later date, add the

canons of the Lateran Council, 1059, and the oath of
Berengarius affirming Transubstantiation. These belong to
the period of the Gregorian Reform and suggest that canon
law in England was developing *pari passu* with developments
on the Continent.

That the full canon law was regarded as binding in England
is now so generally admitted, that it is a waste of time to
argue it. The Provinciale of Lyndwood, chief legal officer
of Archbishop Chichele in the early fifteenth century, is a
text, with learned legal commentary, of the provincial
constitutions of successive Archbishops of Canterbury. It is
not the code of canon law of the English Church. It is a
learned text book expounding one small part of that law,
and that always by reference to the greater whole. The
binding nature of the Decretals is everywhere taken for
granted and the authority of the Archbishops rigidly con-
fined and curtailed by it.

Let me give two examples. (1) A constitution of John
Peckham containes the sentence, "Priests are to be careful,
when giving Communion to the faithful at Easter or at any
other time, to instruct them that the Body and Blood of
Christ are both contained in the species of bread, etc."
Lyndwood[1] comments "at Easter because all adults are then
bound to receive Communion, or 'any other time', i.e.
Whitsun and Christmas, when the secular clergy are bound
to communicate. But as for the laity, they are not required
to communicate except at Easter." His implication is clear:
the Archbishop has no power, and therefore is presumed not to
intend to bind the laity beyond the provisions of the common
law which required Communion once a year only, viz. at
Easter.

(2) A Constitution of Archbishop Chichele prescribes the
manner in which the feast of St. John of Beverley is to be
observed, and requires conformity in this matter to the Sarum
Use. Lyndwood comments that the common law—and he
cites two texts—orders that the use to be followed in any

[1] Oxford Edition, p. 8.

Province is that of the Cathedral of the Metropolis. But in England he says there is a long standing custom that the Sarum Use is the pattern. This is a reasonable custom and therefore it has the sanction of the Common Law: and he refers to a number of texts dealing with "custom" and the ways in which it becomes the law (p. 104).

There were, indeed, other matters in which the canon law in England differed from the canon law in operation on the Continent. These divergences are due to the prevalance of local customs, recognised and allowed for by the "common law". The common law was the Corpus, the law valid for the whole Church: but in different localities particular customs, contrary to the common law, acquired validity and became themselves "the law" on that matter and in that place. The outstanding examples of such local customs acquiring the force of law in England are (1) the right of the spiritual courts to a more extensive jurisdiction in the matter of the probate of wills, (2) *per contra*, the removal of jurisdiction in cases of ecclesiastical patronage from the spiritual courts to the temporal, (3) the responsibility of the owners of rectorial tithes for the maintenance and upkeep of the chancels of parish churches and (4) children born out of wedlock were not held by English courts to be legitimated by the subsequent marriage of their parents, though according to the Corpus they are to be so held.[1]

But the existence of such variations from the common law in no way indicates that pre-Reformation England had a canon law of its own, different from and independent of the canon law of Europe of which we have traced the development. There was but the one Corpus Juris Canonici: its authority was recognised and undisputed throughout Western Christendom. I hope next to try to indicate what became of it in England after the Church of England threw off the jurisdiction of the Pope on whose authority the canon law had come to depend.

[1] See *Marriage in Church and State*, Lacey, ed. Mortimer (S.P.C.K.), p. 123 for details and qualifications.

THE CANON LAW IN ENGLAND
AFTER THE REFORMATION

THE canon law of which we have traced the development down to the formation of the Corpus Juris Canonici was an integral part of English life. It may be said to have been officially authorised in England as part of the law of the land by an ordinance of William the Conqueror. This laid down that no case which concerned the discipline of souls (*quae ad regimen animarum pertinet*) was to be brought before the secular courts, but that all persons cited for any cause or crime covered by the bishops' laws were to be tried by the Bishop *secundum canones et episcopales leges*. This ordinance established two systems of jurisdiction. It was inevitable that they should overlap at points, and that disputes and conflicts should arise over particular issues. But in general the principle went unchallenged that England was a part of Christendom, a unit in a wider society, and that the law of that wider society was valid. As Professor Powicke says, "Human society was one, held together by belief in and obedience to God in a visible Church which comprised all Christian people, but also directed in this life by various kinds of secular authority." (*The Reformation in England*, p. 1.) In other words, Church authorities and Church law—a common system for all Christendom—ruled in matters of faith and morals, expecting and for the most part receiving the full assistance of the secular authorities. These secular authorities were themselves supreme in all other matters.

The repudiation of the Papal supremacy naturally raised an acute problem. For it cut off the canon law from its reputed source, and left it with no authority: for that authority on which it was held to depend was declared to have no

force whatever in England. Henry VIII attempted to solve this problem by two simple devices. He asserted that the place formerly held by the Pope was now occupied by himself. *He* was to be the source and fount of the canon law. Secondly, it was asserted that the canon law had never been operative in England because of the Pope's authority, but simply and solely because it had been freely accepted and taken upon themselves by the English kings and peoples.

In this way Henry VIII converted the canon or Church law into national law. On this theory—which had no foundation in fact—it was the law, not of Christendom, deriving from the head of Christendom, the Pope, but the law of the Church of England, long accepted in this country by the sovereign will of the people, and now declared to be binding, and to derive its authority from the King's Majesty as Head or Governor of the Church in England. Thus the Peter Pence and Dispensation Act (25 Henry VIII, c. 21) contains this clause: "This your Grace's Realm, recognising no superior under God, but only your Grace, has been and is free from subjection to any man's laws, but only to such as have been devised, made and obtained within this realm for the wealth of the same, or to such other as by sufferance of your Grace and his Progenitors, the People of this your Realm have taken at their free liberty, by their own consent to be used among them, and have bound themselves by long use and custom to the observance of the same, not as to the observance of laws of any foreign prince potentate or prelate, but as to the customed and ancient laws of this Realm."

A year previously, in the preamble to the Act in Restraint of Appeals (24 Henry VIII, c. 12) it was stated "The Body Spiritual whereof, having Power when any cause of the law Divine happened to come in question, or of spiritual learning, then it was declared, interpreted and shewed by that part of the said Body Politick called the Spirituality, now being usually called the English Church, which always hath been reputed and also found of that sort that both for knowledge, integrity and sufficiency of number it hath always been thought, and

is also at this hour, sufficient and meet of itself, without the intermeddling of any exterior person or persons to declare and determine all such doubts and to administer all such offices and duties as to their Rooms Spiritual doth pertain." What this means is that the whole canon law, whatever the historical accident of its origin, so far as England is concerned is declared to be a purely English affair. It is English law, and law for the whole of England. In so far as it might stand in need of revision or extension, it should be revised and extended by the English Body Spiritual, under the leave and consent of the King. The act which embodies the submission of the clergy (25 Henry VIII, c. 19) states that the clergy "have promised in verbo sacerdotis that they will never from henceforth presume to attempt allege claim or put in use or enact promulge or execute any new canons, constitutions, ordinances . . . in the Convocations unless the King's most royal assent and licence may to them be had to make promulge or execute the same, and that his Majesty do give his most royal assent and authority in that behalf."

The matter cannot be more clearly stated, even though the statement be somewhat biased and one-sided, than in the words of that most influential lawyer of James I's reign, the Lord Chief Justice, Sir Edward Coke. He summed up the position thus: "By the ancient law of this realm, this kingdom of England is an absolute empire and monarchy, consisting of one head, which is the king, and of a body politic, compact and compounded of many and almost infinite several and yet well agreeing members. All which the law divideth into two general parts, that is to say, the clergy and laity, both of them, next and immediately after God, subject and obedient to the head. Also the kingly head of this politic body is instituted and furnished with plenary and entire power prerogative and jurisdiction to render justice and right to every part and member of this body, of what estate, degree or calling soever, in all causes ecclesiastical or temporal; otherwise he should not be a head of the whole body. And as in temporal causes, the king by the mouth of

his judges in his courts of justice, doth judge and determine
the same by the temporal laws of England, so in causes
ecclesiastical and spiritual . . . the same are to be determined
and decided by judges according to the king's ecclesiastical
laws of this realm." (S. Co. Cawdries case. Burn *Ecclesiastical Law* II, p. 38.)

In speaking thus of the "king's ecclesiastical laws" rather
than of "the canon law" or "the ecclesiastical law" this great
lawyer was, I dare say, being intentionally provocative. He
wished to make clear the effect upon the canon law and
the spiritual courts which administered it, of the Royal
supremacy. In the pre-Reformation days, the kings allowed
that the canon law was binding on their subjects, and on
themselves, at least for the greater part, although they had
had no share in the making of it, and at the most could prevent the publication of isolated enactments. But by the Act
of Submission the clergy had admitted that the canon law
was binding on them and on the country, only by the King's
licence and authority. Without the King's authority it would
not be binding: where it ran directly counter to the King's
authority it was declared to be abolished: and only by the
King's authority could it be changed. There is a real sense,
therefore, in which the canon law, despite its origin, can be
called the King's law. And because it is the King's law it
is binding on every one of the King's subjects. The Reformers
and the Tudor sovereigns had no knowledge of the quaint
conceit which holds the canon law to bind the clergy and not
the laity. On the contrary, they wished to use the canon law
as an instrument for ruling the laity as much and even more
than as a disciplinary weapon over the clergy. The Jacobean
canons of 1604 are aimed as much at schismatic and heretical
and immoral laymen as against the clergy. The King governs
his subjects in part and on some matters through the civil
law and the civil courts, in part and on other matters through
the canon law and the spiritual courts. And when he wishes
to change the law, he acts in the one case through Parliament,
and in the other through the Convocations.

Such I understand to be the nature of the Reformation Establishment. The Establishment itself, not unnaturally, was ratified by Parliament as well as by the Convocations. The Submission of the Clergy in Convocation was embodied in almost identical words in the Act of Submission in Parliament. Both request a revision of the canon law, both state that until that be done the old canon law shall remain in force—the Convocations implicitly, Parliament explicitly. The old canon law, therefore, is binding by Parliamentary statute also. But it was not intended that it should be revised by Parliament. That work was entrusted to a Commission of thirty-two persons appointed by the King, sixteen spiritual and sixteen lay.

After some delay the Commission was appointed and got to work. Its findings, however, were never ratified by the King; in the reign of Edward VI Parliament again authorised the setting up of a Commission (3 and 4 Edward VI, c. 11) and this time eight persons were appointed with instructions to complete the work within three years. This they failed to do, and for some reason or other an extension of the period had not been granted by the time that Edward VI died. During the reign of Mary and the Roman Catholic reaction, the matter dropped. In the reign of Elizabeth it was again suggested that the work of revision should be resumed and finished, and it appears that Archbishop Parker did actually finish it, and allow, if he did not authorise, its publication in book form. But the Queen, disliking and distrusting, as it seems, the meddling by Parliament in ecclesiastical affairs, stopped Parliament's discussion of the book. With that decision all idea of a complete and general revision of the canon law in England ceased.[1]

At no point was this general revision ever ratified by Convocation. It has, therefore, never had the slightest authority. It is, however, an extremely interesting book. It is called "Reformatio Legum Ecclesiasticarum". In many

[1] For the details of the history see Strype Cranmer I, 388 pp. and Parker II, 62 pp. and Cardwell *Reform of Ecclesiastical Laws*, Preface.

places it reveals the powerful impact upon England of the spirit of the Continental Reformation—particularly in the section dealing with marriage, where the ideas of the Dutch Reformers find expression. Characteristic of these ideas is the provision that the innocent party to a divorce is allowed to re-marry, the guilty partner is sentenced to life-long exile or imprisonment. Still, in spite of such blemishes, the book is a skilful attempt to reduce to some sort of order a great portion of the old mediaeval law and it represents the considered opinion of authority in the sixteenth century as to what part of the old law it was desirable to retain.

This attempt at a general revision having failed, the content and authority of the canon law now rests on the wording of the Act of Parliament which ordered the revision (25 Henry VIII, c. 19), namely "that such canons, etc. being already made which be not contrariant or repugnant to the laws, statutes and customs of the Realm, nor to the damage or hurt of the King's Prerogative Royal, shall still now be used and executed as they were afore the making of this act." This still holds.

The year 1571 which saw the failure of the Reformatio Legum Ecclesiasticarum, produced a short series of canons subscribed by the Upper Houses of Canterbury and York. Lacking the signatures of the Lower Houses and the ratification of the Queen, they have no sort of binding authority. Yet they are interesting as showing the freedom allowed at this time to Convocation, and because they form the basis of the later canons of 1604. A further series of thirteen Articles "touching the admission of apt and fit persons to the ministry and the establishing of good orders in the Church" were drawn up by the Convocation of Canterbury in 1575 and authorised by the Queen. A similar series with the same authority was issued in 1585. A rather longer series in the same way was authorised in 1597. All of these were revised and new canons added in 1604. These last canons, 141 in number, drawn up by Convocation and ratified by the King, have full and absolute validity. They are in no sense

a code of canon law. But within a certain strictly limited area they represent a most important effort by the Church of England at canonical legislation. They are, of course, by now largely obsolete and it is on their revision that the Church of England is now engaged. In 1640 the two Convocations framed further canons, with a view to supporting the King's cause against Parliament, to suppressing Papists and Sectaries (for which end an oath was imposed on the higher clergy) and to enforcing certain rites and ceremonies. These canons were subscribed to by both houses of both Convocations and received the royal assent. They were, formally, completely valid: but their unpopularity was so great, and they were so soon followed by the disasters of the Civil War, that they never became operative. They so enraged the House of Commons that it passed a resolution "that the clergy of England convented in any Convocation . . . have no power to make any constitutions, canons or acts whatsoever . . . without common consent of parliament". (Quoted Cardwell Synodalia I, p. 385, note.) This was the last attempt by the Convocations to frame new canons on any considerable scale. In 1866, 1887, 1892, 1921, 1933, 1936 and 1946 various particular canons of the 1604 series were amended.

The canon law, then, of the Church of England is the old mediaeval law, except where it has been altered by subsequent Acts of Parliament or by those activities of the Convocations which I have just listed, to which should be added their doctrinal and liturgical work. A concise, although not complete picture of the general scope of the canon law is given by Sir Edward Coke in the passage which I have already quoted. He says, ". . . so in causes ecclesiastical and spiritual, as namely blasphemy, apostacy from Christianity, heresies, schisms, ordering, admissions, institutions of clerks, celebration of divine service, rights of matrimony, divorces, general bastardy, subtraction and right of tithes, oblations, obventions, dilapidations, reparation of churches, probate of testaments, administrations and accounts upon the same,

simony, incests, fornications, adulteries, solicitations of chastity, pensions, procurations, appeals in ecclesiastical causes, commutations of penance and others, (the cognisance whereof belongeth not to the common laws of England) the same are to be determined and decided by ecclesiastical judges, according to the King's ecclesiastical laws of this realm."

Very considerable inroads have been made upon all this by Parliament, both in respect to the law and to the powers of the ecclesiastical courts. It is probably true that Parliament cannot touch the canon law itself. But its own legislative enactments, backed by superior force, can make the canon law of no effect. By transferring to the civil courts what formerly belonged to the spiritual—both causes and persons —and prohibiting the spiritual courts from exercising some of their functions it has restricted the canon law to a comparatively small area. And even within that area, by its own legislation, it has laid down rules and prescribed procedures which have driven the canon law into disuse. The modern position is thus wholly different from that of the Tudor Establishment. Any reform of the canon law must take account of that, as also of the fact that many of the Parliamentary acts are of a kind which Convocation itself would have been well advised to pass, had it had the opportunity. Indeed many of the Parliamentary Acts were passed at the explicit request of the Church. It is not a matter of simple domination of the State over the Church or of unwarranted interference. I propose very briefly to rehearse the changes which have been effected in some parts of the field.

In the first place the competence of the ecclesiastical courts has been considerably reduced by the abolition [final and complete in the reign of George IV (7 and 8 George IV, c. 28)] of the benefit of clergy. No one, I imagine, desires to see restored the exclusive right of the Church courts to try all clerks accused of breaches of the criminal law of the land. The whole mass of canonical legislation which records the various agreements with the State for the handing over of clerks accused of criminal offences from the civil to the

E

spiritual courts, and which governs their trials and convictions there, may now properly be struck out.

Secondly, the system of tithes has been abolished by an Act of Parliament (26 George V and Edward VIII, c. 43). By this another vast section of the canon law has become otiose. The Church of England has, really, now no *law* about the duty and obligation of the laity to contribute towards the maintenance of the Church and her Ministry. There is much exhortation, and much Diocesan machinery for the collection of voluntary gifts, but there is no law. No tithes and no church rates can be levied and collected with the help of the civil power. There is, here, a real gap which ought to be filled. There should be, at the least, a simple canon enjoining on the laity the duty of contributing to the support of the Church and leaving the amount to be assessed by each individual conscience. Or, alternatively, and perhaps less desirably, there should be canons enjoining as a condition of Church membership the payment of a fixed percentage of income, and providing machinery for its collection.

Thirdly, Parliament, by an act of 1857, has withdrawn from the ecclesiastical courts the right and duty of supervising and administering the probate of wills. (20 and 21 Victoria. c. 77.) By this another large section of the canon law has passed out of use. I do not suppose that anyone seriously wishes to see it revived.

Fourthly, Parliament in the same year withdrew from the ecclesiastical courts all questions concerning the validity of marriage contracts, the legitimacy of issue, and the granting of orders of separation. The preliminaries of marriage, banns and licences, and the contract itself are now governed by the canon or the civil law indifferently, at the discretion of the parties. This is a sphere and a large and important sphere, where the canon law retains its efficacy. It has been modified in some details by Statute law, but the main principles and the general mode of working still remain as under the old canon law.

On the main question of the control of marriage laws by

the State rather than by the Church, in so far as only temporal issues are involved—such as the ownership and inheritance of property, or rights of citizenship—the Church may well regard with equanimity this diminution of her control. Neither in any revision of the canon law would the Church claim any exclusive power over all matrimonial causes irrespective of Church membership. Yet where moral questions are involved, and in particular where the permanence of the marriage contract is brought in question, the position is more delicate. On the illegality of marriage after divorce, on those conditions and factors which do and those which do not render a marriage contract null and void, the canon law is clear and explicit. On these matters the Church's marriage laws are neither out-moded nor obscurantist; they are in the main in agreement with the will of God, and more conducive to the moral and spiritual well-being of the people, than are the marriage laws of Parliament. So far at least as her own members are concerned the Church will insist that on such matters she shall legislate herself.

Fifthly, all matters relating to dilapidations, sale and exchange of parsonages, restoration and repair of churches, upkeep of burial grounds, etc., have been under constant revision by Parliament during the last one hundred years. The existing regulations for the most part derive from Parliamentary Acts sponsored by the Church Assembly. Difficulties arise here not from the lack of revision of the old law but from an excess of it. In general, it may perhaps be said, excessive modern reforming zeal has only succeeded in obscuring and confusing the principles of the canon law, without greatly simplifying its procedure.

Sixthly, the rights of patronage, admissions to benefices, resignations and pensions stand in the same position. Here also the experimental efforts of the Church Assembly to bring the old canon law up to date need reviewing and simplifying. Above all the complicated question of the "parson's freehold" requires a careful examination. But in general, over this sphere the old canon law still holds good, and is in force.

Seventhly, the discretionary powers of the bishop in matters
of ordination and licences to officiate appear to be still
governed by the Mediaeval canon law and the Canons of
1604. These might certainly be reviewed, but it is not clear
that any alterations are required. The appointment and
status of stipendiary curates are now regulated by Acts of
Parliament. [Pluralities Act 1838 (122 Victoria, c. 106)
Pluralities Acts, Amendment Act (48 and 49 Victoria,
c. 54), Benefices Act 1898 (61 and 62 Victoria, c. 48).]

So far we have dealt with the administrative sections of the
canon law. We now come to the disciplinary sections which
prescribe moral rules of behaviour and penalites for their
infraction. And, first, the discipline of the clergy.

In questions of morals the procedure before the spiritual
courts is governed by the Church Discipline Act of 1840
(3 and 4 Victoria, c. 86), the Clergy Discipline Act of 1892
(55 and 56 Victoria, c. 32), and the Incumbents (Discipline
and Disability) Measures 1947 and 1945. These various acts
all attempt to define more precisely the conduct condemned
by the 1604 canons, numbers 75 and 109, and to prescribe
the conditions under which clerks may be suspended or
deprived. The intention of the Acts seems to be to make it
easier to deprive unsuitable clerks of their benefices, whilst
at the same time restricting the powers of the bishops. The
attempts have not been successful, and it is high time that
the principles of the canon law were re-asserted, whereby
the bishop, after full and proper trial, has absolute power
to suspend or deprive, in accordance with rules prescribed
by the canons.

The discipline of the clergy in matters involving doctrine
and ritual and the conduct of divine service is governed by
the principles contained in the 39 Articles, the Prayer Book
and the Canons of 1604. All of these carry the authority of
Convocation, and the first two that of Parliament as well.
This section of canon law, all of it post-Reformation, is both
vigorously alive and in confusion. Revision is overdue and
imperative, especially in the spheres of ritual and divine

service. Unfortunately revision is here particularly difficult because of acute divisions within the Church. The administration of discipline in this section is for the most part governed by the Public Worship Regulation Act of 1872. (37 and 38 Victoria, c. 85.)

In all cases of clerical discipline the final Court of Appeal is the Judicial Committee of the Privy Council, with certain ecclesiastical persons acting as assessors. This has proved to be a major source of offence to a large section of the clergy, and has perhaps contributed more than any other single cause to the general indifference to the law and neglect of the spiritual courts in all matters concerning worship and ritual. It is worth while recalling that when Henry VIII first abolished appeals to Rome he made the Archbishop's court the final court, except in certain matters in which an appeal lay to the upper house of Convocation. (24 Henry VIII, c. 12.) It was not until the nineteenth century that it was finally ruled that this appellate jurisdiction of the upper house of Convocation had been abolished by Henry's later legislation. (Gorham v. Exeter (Bishop) 1849–50.) The confused position arising from the multiplicity of courts and procedures caused by the legislation of the last hundred years is now under revision. It is to be hoped that one single and simple judicial system will be established with a court of final appeal at its head commanding general support and loyalty.

The disciplinary and penal character of the canon law in regard to both clergy and laity has its roots, as we have seen, in the old Celtic and Anglo-Saxon penitential system. By that system confessors inflicted heavy penalties in the form of fines, pilgrimages, flagellations and imprisonments on those guilty of moral or criminal offences. These penalties, originally devised for and applied to semi-barbaric races, found their way into the canon law and survived the system which gave them birth. As the canon law was accepted, so it was recognised that the Church had the right and duty in this way of suppressing and punishing wickedness and vice, and of keep-

ing the country free from heretical and corrupting doctrines.
This penal jurisdiction, even over the laity, to some extent
still survives, though for the most part it has been abolished
by Parliament. I propose to run through the main divisions
of this penal discipline.

A. *Heresy.* Canons 5 and 110 of 1604 order heretics to be
cited into the Bishop's court and to be punished "according
to such ecclesiastical laws as are prescribed in that behalfe".
In the reign of James I two cases of the burning of heretics
are recorded. In each case the heretic was sentenced in the
Bishop's court and the writ *de haeretico comburendo* was issued
by the King. Where this drastic action was not taken, the sentence of excommunication pronounced by the Bishop's
court led to the arrest of the heretic by the civil authorities
and to imprisonment or fines. The infliction of the death
penalty as a consequence of any condemnation in an ecclesiastical court was definitely declared illegal in the reign of
Charles II. (29 Charles II, c. 9.) William and Mary prohibited the institution of proceedings for heresy against the
members of any recognised dissenting body. (1 William and
Mary, c. 18.) Apart from this, it appears that presentations
in the Courts can still be made, even against laymen, for
heresy and schism under the 1604 canons. But none now are.

B. *Blasphemy*, which technically includes such activities as
those of the Rationalist Society or the Anti-God propaganda
of Communists, is now an offence against the common law.
It still remains, however, a cause for presentation into the
Bishop's court. But owing to the growth of the spirit of toleration, proceedings are never now taken in either the civil or
spiritual courts.

C. *Simony*, concerning which there are very numerous
regulations in the old canon law, was first made actionable
in the civil courts in the reign of Queen Elizabeth. (31 Elizabeth, c. 6.) From that time it has been possible to try the
offence in either the civil or the ecclesiastical court. The
offence has been more closely defined in various Victorian
Parliamentary Statutes, notably the Clerical Subscription

Act 1865 (29 and 30 Victoria, c. 122) and the Benefices Act 1898 (61 and 62 Victoria, c. 48). It would appear that actions against Patrons and Bishops are always now brought before the civil courts. Against Patrons, I suppose, because it is primarily a question of property, against Bishops because the canon law contains no precise rules or machinery for disciplining bishops, as was shown by the case of Bishop King of Lincoln. Actions against the clergy are heard by the ecclesiastical court set up by the Church Discipline Measure 1840. (3 and 4 Victoria, c. 86.) The penalty is the penalty of the old canon law—all simoniacal contracts are void, all simoniacal ordinations are irregular. State interference here has only resulted in a tightening up of the law in what is probably a salutary manner. Undoubted abuses have been swept away. Little revision is probably needed.

D. *Defamation.* By the old law it was open to anyone to bring an action for defamation in the spiritual courts if he sought no damages for himself, but only the recantation of the slander and the shaming of the slanderer. The scope of the right was gradually limited to cases where the slander alleged an offence itself punishable in the ecclesiastical courts. For example, if a man were called a thief he could not bring an action in the ecclesiastical court, he could sue only in the civil courts; because the spiritual courts have no jurisdiction over theft. By a Victorian Statute (18 and 19 Victoria, c. 41) all suits of this kind, no matter what the slander, were withdrawn from the ecclesiastical courts. No one is likely to regret this or to seek to revive this part of the canon law. The confusion which existed towards the end is admirably illustrated by a case cited by Godolphin.[1] A man was convicted in the Court of Arches for calling another man's wife "Welch Jade" and "Welch Rogue". He appealed to the Court of Audience. It then appeared that he was also accused of calling the woman a "Welch Thief". This nearly led to a dismissal of the whole proceedings, "for it was held clearly that for the word Welch thief action lies at the

[1] Repertorium Canonicum, p. 522: 17

Common law, and they ought not to sue in the Spiritual
Court". And in any case it was held that the other words
were words "only of heat and no slander" and therefore not
actionable in the Spiritual Court. However, it was afterwards
proved that the word "Welch Thief" had been fraudulently
inserted into the pleadings without the plaintiff's knowledge,
and that "Welch Jade" in an ecclesiastical court has the
meaning of "Welch Whore", and that is actionable in the
Spiritual court. And so the appeal failed.

E. *Offences against Sexual Morality*. Offences of this kind,
such as the Prayer Book means by "notorious evil-living"
and Canon 109 calls, "Adultery, whoredom, incest . . . and
other uncleanness and wickedness of life" were the subject
of frequent actions in the ecclesiastical courts, and in fact
Canon 109 lays it upon the Churchwardens as a duty to
bring cases of this kind in to the Bishop's court. It does not
appear that they have ever been relieved of this duty, except
in so far as it is held that no layman is bound by any canon.
They have certainly not been relieved of the right of acting
under the canon, should they so wish. However, for one
reason or another no proceedings have been taken under the
canon for well over a hundred years. The reasons probably
are (1) that the worst offences are covered by special acts of
the State criminal law. (2) That alternative proceedings
against the Clergy are provided by the Clergy Discipline
Act of 1840. (3) That public opinion is more tolerant of such
offences, other than those covered by the criminal law, and
(4) and chiefly that the Churchwardens themselves shrink
from the publicity involved.

It is clear that this disciplinary system can never have
been popular, and it may be wondered how it was enforced.
Why did a layman when presented by the Churchwardens
answer to the summons of the Spiritual Courts? He sub-
mitted to the threat of excommunication. Those who did not
obey the orders of the Court were excommunicated, and the
Court applied to the King's Court for a writ *de excommunicato
capiendo*. This writ had to be issued on application and it

then became the business of the King's Officers to arrest the person named. This procedure, which goes back behind the Reformation, was in some details revised and re-enforced by Elizabeth. (5 Elizabeth, c. 23.) It is a most remarkable example of the support of the Church by the State. Furthermore, excommunication, the Church's chief weapon of punishment, carried with it severe civil disabilities. An excommunicated person might not bring an action in a court of law or practice at the bar or give evidence; he might not make a will, nor be buried in consecrated ground; though he might be appointed an executor or receive a legacy, he could not claim the legacy nor prove the will in court. All this lasted till the reign of George III. It was then in great part abolished by Statute. (53 George III, c. 127.) The Spiritual Courts were forbidden to pronounce a sentence of excommunication as a means of procuring the attendance of cited persons before them or of punishing any contempt of Court. In place of the writ *de excommunicato capiendo*, a writ *de contumace capiendo* was issued. This had the same intention and effect, of enforcing the jurisdiction of the spiritual courts, but avoided the cheapening and the degradation of the supreme canonical penalty of excommunication which the older system involved. Excommunication itself was also shorn by this Statute of its civil consequences. The worst thing which could happen, civilly, to an excommunicated person was six months' imprisonment. This Act has undoubtedly restored to excommunication its proper spiritual character. The canon law still retains the penalty of excommunication itself, and in my judgement it is still within the competence of a Spiritual Court to inflict it on both clergy and laity—at any rate in principle. In practice, for what precise offences it could be imposed on a layman is, to me, far from clear. The matter is closely connected with the ruling that the canons of 1603 only bind the laity in so far as they are declaratory of the ancient pre-Reformation usage and law. The possible resumption by the Spiritual Courts of an active use of the penalty of excommunication is likely

to prove one of the liveliest bones of contention when the new revised canons of the Church of England come up for public discussion.

This very incomplete review of the subject matter of the canon law will have made it clear how constantly it has been modified by Acts of Parliament. This fact has robbed the Convocations of much of their freedom in any work of revision. For the Act of Submission of the Clergy bound the Convocations not to make promulge or execute any canons without the Royal Licence. Further, even if the Royal Licence and Assent be obtained, the canons would still be void and without effect if (a) they were against the Royal Prerogative, (b) against the common law, (c) against the Statute law, or (d) against any custom of the Realm. It is clear, therefore, that in England any extensive legislative activity by the Church would require the co-operation of Parliament in order to overcome these several barriers, particularly in the matter of over-riding or amending the many Parliamentary modifications and adaptations of the old canon law. This difficulty was felt as far back as the days of Archbishop Sandys who complained to Queen Elizabeth in 1585 of a proposed bill in Parliament about the qualifications to be required of men seeking ordination that it "besides other inconveniences (as namely, the trial of the minister's sufficiency by twelve laymen and such like) hath this also, that if it pass by Parliament, it cannot hereafter but in Parliament be altered, what necessity soever shall urge thereunto. . . . Whereas if it is but as a canon from us by your Majesty's authority, it may be observed or altered at your pleasure."

In its present work of revision, therefore, the Church of England is faced with difficulties which do not exist for other branches of the Anglican Communion—except in parts of Australia. Elsewhere ecclesiastical legislative authorities are free to amend or adapt their canons in such ways as they think wise and expedient, and the procedure is relatively simple. However, we are in great hopes in England that our difficulties will be overcome. We believe that there is a grow-

ing recognition that the role of Parliament to represent the laity and to protect their rights in ecclesiastical matters is now obsolescent and has passed into the hands of the House of Laity of the Church Assembly. We believe also that there is an increased willingness on the part of Parliament to grant the Church a fuller freedom to order her own life and to discipline her members; we believe indeed that there is a better understanding that without such freedom the Church herself is weakened, her influence and hold over the Nation is decreased and the good of the whole country is threatened. We hope and believe that a revised form of the Establishment will come in this generation—a form wherein the Church, renewed and re-invigorated will prove a willing and effective partner of the State in promoting the true well-being of the people. It is to that end that our present efforts to revise the Canon Law are directed.

V

THE CHARACTERISTICS OF CANON LAW

THE law of the Church is concerned not only, and indeed perhaps not primarily, with the good of the Church as a Society, but rather with the good of each individual member. And the good of the individual which it seeks to promote is not a temporal good, but his eternal welfare. It is natural, therefore, that the canon law should show certain peculiar features of its own. There are four on which I propose to touch in this lecture; they are (1) the sharply-drawn distinction between that part of the law which is invariable and admits of no alteration or exceptions, and that part which is subject to change in accordance with the varying conditions of time and place; (2) arising out of that, the respect accorded in the canon law to local custom and (3) the flexibility shown in applying the law to individuals. The fourth point concerns the treatment of offences and the character of ecclesiastical punishment.

The distinction between the variable and the immutable parts of the canon law is very clearly drawn by Ivo of Chartres in his Prologue. It is based on the distinction between laws which are held to be of divine origin and those which are of purely ecclesiastical authority. Here are his words, "Some laws are changeable, some are not. Unchangeable laws are those which are sanctioned by eternal law, the observance of which assures salvation ... such as 'Thou shalt love the Lord thy God'. Changeable laws are those which are not sanctioned by eternal law, but which have been invented by the wisdom of the elders, not for the procuring of salvation but for its preservation. Unchangeable laws are directed against vices: they lay down the minimum necessary to salvation. Changeable laws do not prohibit things bad in

themselves, but are aids and precautions. And so ecclesiastical law should be interpreted charitably provided that nothing is done contrary to the Gospel and the Apostles. . . . In those matters on the observance of which salvation depends, no dispensation is possible: such prohibitions or precepts are to be kept absolutely, as being sanctioned by eternal law. But rules made for disciplinary purposes can on occasion be dispensed, for a just cause." This is no new doctrine, invented by Ivo. Augustine had said that customs may vary from place to place, but nothing may be done which is contrary to faith and morals. (Ep. 54. Migne, P. L., 33/210.) Leo the Great had said that there are some things which can never be altered, but others which may be adjusted for considerations of necessity or of age, provided that it be always rememberd that in doubtful matters nothing must be done contrary to the precepts of the Gospel and the decrees of the Fathers. (Ep. 90.)

In consequence we find that part of the canon law is characterised by an extreme rigidity, and part by a remarkable flexibility. The distinction runs right back to the New Testament and St. Paul's "to the married I command, yet not I but the Lord" and his "but to the rest speak I, not the Lord". That which is of divine origin is immutable, that which is of ecclesiastical is mutable. But whilst the distinction itself has been constant, the history of canon law shows a continuous shifting of the dividing line between the two parts. In many cases there has been an extreme difficulty in deciding whether a particular law is or is not of divine origin. Perhaps the clearest example is that of the prohibited degrees of kindred and affinity. Is the prohibition of marrying a deceased wife's sister of divine origin or not? For many centuries it was held that it was, and under no circumstances was any such marriage allowed. Gradually the contrary opinion gained ground, that the prohibition was not really of divine origin but a part of purely human law. Consequently such marriages might, at least on occasion, be allowed. The history of this may be found in any competent book on the

canon law of marriage, e.g. Esmein *Marriage en Droit Canonique*
or in *Kindred and Affinity* (S.P.C.K., Report of Archbishops'
Commission).

In general it may, I think, be said that apart from fundamental moral precepts the most important part of the immutable canon law concerns the validity of the Sacraments. The
Sacraments are nothing if they are not of divine origin: the
conditions which are clearly laid down by God concerning
their administration the Church cannot alter. The only room
for change here lies in the Church's judicial power to determine what those conditions are. Her determinations in this
sphere constitute the matter, form and minister essential to
the valid administration of a Sacrament. And these determinations no individual and no subordinate authority can
alter. Moreover these determinations themselves form no
part of the Church's legislative function: they are not rules
or orders which the Church has made, and which the Church
can therefore alter. They are judgements of fact, of what
God has ordained: they are akin to the Church's doctrinal
Statements, which are also judgements of fact, of the truths
which God has actually revealed. The only change possible
is through an added precision given to these determinations
in order to prevent or deny any misunderstandings or per-
versions which may have arisen.

The mutable canon law, which is indeed the greater part,
is that body of laws and regulations by which the Church is
ordered, and by which their respective rights and duties are
assigned to the different kinds of members. These laws are
only immutable when and in so far as they contain or express
some precept of the divine or natural law. Thus the canon
will lay down the minimum age at which a man may be
ordained to the priesthood, and the moral, physical and in-
tellectual qualifications which he must have. But any of this
may be altered from time to time or even to meet particular
cases. That the candidate for ordination must be a man and
not a woman, however, admits of no alteration or exception,
because that is part of the determination by the Church of

what is divinely required for the validity of the Sacrament of Orders. Again the canons will contain a great number of regulations about the solemnisation of matrimony. Most of these are mutable: but many are not, because they are a part of "natural law". Thus no exception is possible to the canon forbidding a man to marry his mother, for such a marriage is totally forbidden by the divine, or natural, prohibition of incest. Nor is an exception possible to the canon forbidding a man to have two wives. For that is polygamy.

The mutable canon law is the expression of the legislative authority of the Church imposing upon her members the obligation to do particular things in a particular way. Thus the Church prescribes a universal obligation to fast, and further determines the times and manner of fasting. And this she will do from time to time in accordance with what she thinks most conducive to the spiritual end of fasting. Or again, she will determine her organisation into provinces, dioceses and parishes: she will arrange how such existing units may have their boundaries altered, how fresh such units may be brought into being. She will determine how and by whom bishops and parish priests are to be appointed, and, when appointed, what are their rights and duties. We have seen that that was an important part of the classical canon law, which insisted on one bishop, with or without assistants, in control of each diocese, and on one parish priest, with or without assistants, in charge of each parish, under and by institution from the bishop. These are general provisions, establishing the major frame-work. It is not, I think, desirable that they should be altered. But they could be, and they sometimes have been, e.g. the organisation of the Celtic Church was markedly different from the "classical" frame-work. Yet within that frame-work there is a multitude of minor regulations which have been and ought to be altered from time to time as the Church or any part of the Church judges the spiritual well-being of her members to require.

Throughout the mutable part of the canon law, the overriding consideration is the spiritual well-being of the members

of Christ's Body, of how best in any age or place the people may be enabled to serve and worship God. It is obvious that what is well conceived for the Church as a whole may fit ill with some particular local conditions: or what is good for one age or place may become a hindrance under changed conditions. Hence it is that the canon law pays such respect to local customs, which have grown up under local conditions and which express the mind of the local church on how best the cause of God may be served in her special conditions. Custom is the continuously expressed will of the people: the emergence and growth of local custom is, generally speaking, a sign of vigorous life.

A custom may develop in some matter concerning which the law is silent (*praeter legem*). If it satisfies certain conditions, it comes to exercise obligatory force, and is indeed part of the law. For example, in England the custom has developed in relatively recent times of having special services for Mothering Sunday and the Harvest Festival. There is, in England, no written law requiring these. But they have now become customary and any incumbent who refused to hold them might reasonably be convicted of negligence. More interesting are those customs which develop in direct opposition to the written law (*contra legem*). An ancient example of this in England is the custom by which the Rector (i.e. the owner of the tithe) was responsible for the repair and maintenance of the chancel of the Parish church. The general law of the Western Church was that the people were responsible for the fabric of the whole church. But this contrary custom developed in England, so that in the end the people could disclaim any responsibility for the chancel and the Rector could be legally compelled to maintain it. Another example is that Rural Deans, in England, are appointed by the Bishop. But in the Diocese of Exeter they are, by custom, elected. How it came about, I do not know; I suppose that in Exeter it was commonly thought that that was the better way. A custom may be negative: that is, it may consist in a non-observance or continued disobedience of some law. Thus

the canons in England still say that the clergy are to wear their cassocks out of doors. But the custom of not doing so is now so well established that the canon requiring it has lost its obligatory force. But perhaps the outstanding example of the development of a custom in modern England is that of the wearing of eucharistic vestments. In the face of a declaration of their illegality and in spite of prolonged opposition by authority, their revived use persisted and the custom has so far established itself that it is proposed in the new canons that their use be explicitly recognised as lawful.

But it must not be supposed that any custom automatically establishes itself as part of the law. For that, certain conditions must be satisfied. In the first place, the custom must be "reasonable". That is, it must be a good custom, not a bad one. And it must not only not be actually bad, but it must positively conduce to some good, it must serve some useful purpose. In the second place the custom must be continuously observed over a specific period—usually forty years. And thirdly, the custom must have the consent of the legislative authority. If the custom is frequently and expressly denounced by authority, it cannot establish itself. The consent of authority need not, however, be explicit: it may be given tacitly by the mere fact of tolerating it and refraining from any active opposition to it.

Customs which thus develop in addition to or contrary to the requirements of the written law may obtain either obligatory or permissive force; that is, in the former case, they may impose a new obligation binding on everyone: in the latter case they allow a practice, without fear of prosecution for either doing it or not doing it. To give an example of the former, it is customary in England for girls and women to wear veils at their Confirmation. There is, however, no written law which requires this. Yet I think that, if a bishop so wished, he could now, on the strength of the custom, require everyone to do so. An example of a custom acquiring only a permissive force is provided by the use in England of eucharistic vestments. The effect of the custom has been that

F

their use is permissible, it is not compulsory. The result of any such permissive custom is to remove some existing obligation to do something, so that one is free either to do it or not; or to remove some existing prohibition so that one is free now to do what was formerly forbidden, but is not required to do it.

The growth and development of customs gives a great flexibility to the canon law. Customs are the means by which, short of or prior to express legislation, the law adapts itself to changing circumstances. Customs sometimes have their origin in deliberate disobedience and self-will. Authority is wilfully defied. Sometimes they start with an honest conviction that a particular law is outmoded and obedience to it does more harm than good. Authority is disobeyed, regretfully but under the compulsion of a sense of duty. But whether the custom starts in good faith or in bad makes no difference, if it be later approved by the Church. This possibility of the development of custom is largely due to the third characteristic of canon law which I wish to mention—its flexibility in applying the law to individuals.

The authorities upon whom the responsibility of administering the canon law is laid have one supreme over-ruling purpose—the good of souls. They are not primarily concerned with the enforcement of the law as such: they demand obedience only in so far as obedience is in the interests of the soul's health. In most branches of law the officers are concerned to see that the law is obeyed, and they have little, if any, option or discretion in its application. It is not for them to allow exceptions beforehand or to exonerate them afterwards. The law is the law and they must enforce it. But laws are necessarily general: they are just and reasonable in normal circumstances. In abnormal circumstances, however, they may apply only with difficulty and hardship. In canon law more than in any other branch of law account is taken of this limitation, and means are provided whereby the law may be applied with greater justice and precision to individual cases. The instrument employed is that of dispensa-

tion. To this we must now turn our attention for a moment. The canon law gives to the appropriate superior the power to exempt, for a good and sufficient reason, a particular individual from the obligation of a particular law. First, we will consider the reason. This is, in the long run, always the same—that to apply the law in this case would be harmful, but to make an exception would do good. The harm and the good involved may be that of the whole Church, or that of a great number of people, or that of one particular person only. The more important the law to which it is suggested that an exception be made, the greater must be the reason for it. That is obvious. Because if a law is very important, that means that the general well-being of the Church or of an individual depends to a considerable extent on its being observed. In that case any exception is likely to do great harm. In consequence, to justify the exception some great advantage must be expected or some particularly grievous harm be avoided in this individual case.

For example: (1) It is obviously in the interests of the Church that a parish priest should reside in his parish and carry out his duties personally. Consequently the canons enjoin such residence and render non-resident clergy liable to severe penalties. But it can happen that in some circumstances a strict application of this rule would be injurious to the Church or would involve serious hardship to a particular priest. For instance, and this was a common occurence in the Middle Ages, the parish priest may desire to resume his studies at the university and acquire a specialist expertness in some branch of theology; the Church would benefit by his doing so. It is not difficult to think of other grounds which would justify a more or less lengthy absence in the interests of the Church. Or again, from the point of view of the good of an individual, the lack of a suitable house or the great expense of providing one in a particular district might make a strict application of the law of residence in the parish unduly onerous. In all such cases the system of dispensations provides a valuable flexibility.

(2) It is clearly in the interests of the Church, that as a rule no priest should occupy more than one benefice: in general the duties of any one benefice are enough to occupy his full attention. It is equally obvious that circumstances will not infrequently arise which will make the strict application of this rule disadvantageous: for example, a shortage of clergy, or a deficiency of stipend. In consequence, the canons both expressly forbid pluralities and make provision, by way of a dispensation, for exceptions.

(3) It is a wise precaution which insists that no marriage shall be solemnized before, by a public announcement, any objectors have been invited to come forward and state their objections. This necessarily involves some delay, and the publicity may sometimes be injurious to the parties in ways which have nothing to do with the validity or invalidity of the proposed marriage. The calling of banns is the simplest and easiest way of making sure through publicity that there are no impediments to a marriage. But it is not the only way. In consequence the canons require that normally the banns shall be called, but provision is made for a licence, that is, a dispensation—to dispense with banns and rely on the oath of the parties—in special cases.

It is of greater importance to the Church as a whole that the rules about Residence and Pluralities should be generally obeyed, than it is that there should be due publicity before marriages. It is right, therefore, that in those two cases it should be more difficult than in the third to get a dispensation, that a stronger reason must be advanced and that fewer dispensations should in fact be given. For there is no doubt that a dispensation is—what for centuries it has been described as being—"a wound of the law". The granting of a dispensation does tend of itself, *ipso facto*, to encourage the granting of further dispensations, and so to the final establishment of what is almost a custom of granting them, and the creation of a quasi right to them. And all this in spite of the strictest precautions taken by the canon law to prevent it.

The law lays it down that a dispensation is always a par-

ticular favour, granted to particular applicants for particular reasons. It creates no precedent and establishes no rights for others. No one can claim a dispensation because one has been granted to somebody else in what appear to be similar circumstances. Each dispensation is, in theory, a single and isolated act. Its effect is to repeal the law in regard to its application in one particular case, so that there ceases, in that one case, to be any obligation to obey the law and so that the normal consequences of disobedience in that case do not follow. For example, whilst a marriage contracted simply without publication of banns is invalid, a marriage after licence—i.e. after a dispensation from calling banns—is valid. And if the circumstances or causes for which the dispensation was granted cease to exist or are substantially changed, the dispensation is brought to an end and the obligation to obey the law recurs. For example, a dispensation from fasting granted on account of illness ceases with the illness: a dispensation from residence on the ground that there is no parsonage house ceases when a house is built or provided. Moreover, the dispensing authorities are constantly reminded and enjoined that they must not grant dispensations without good and sufficient cause.

Nevertheless, in spite of these precautions, dispensations do tend to become customary and quasi-automatic: special licences of marriage without publication of banns are a clear example of this. It has become a simple matter, almost, of buying them. At the time of the Reformation the abuses connected with the granting of dispensations were notorious, and a source of grave danger to the Church. A drastic tightening up and restriction in the matter of dispensations was one of the features of the counter-Reformation in the Church of Rome—the discussions and canons of the Council of Trent are evidence enough. In the Reformed Churches the memory of the abuses was so strong that the whole system was severely deprecated and an effort made to do without it altogether, or at least—as in England—to reduce it to the barest minimum. Yet, in my opinion, some such

system—for all its danger—is necessary to the well-being of the Church. It must be made possible somehow to adapt laws of general application to the special needs of individual cases, and by such easy flexibility to cause them to attain their proper end; that is, to subserve in all instances the spiritual good of each soul and the welfare of the Church. If there is no such system, then the law itself becomes from time to time a stone of stumbling to the little ones of Christ.

It is a matter of some importance in whose hands lies the authority to grant dispensations. The Mediaeval Canonists, elaborating the doctrine of the Papal supremacy, had little difficulty in establishing that the sole fount of such authority is the Pope himself. Others, they held, may grant dispensations only in so far as they are authorised by him to do so. This was not, of course, the earlier theory or practice. Before the universal jurisdiction of the Pope was recognised, the normal dispensing authority was the Diocesan Bishops. They lost this independent power to the Pope only gradually. And they lost it through the general acceptance of the legal maxim that "he has power to dispense from a law who has power to make the law". As the Pope was held to be the sole legislator, the power of the Bishops to dispense in their own right necessarily disappeared.

Yet there is something to be said for the view that the granting of dispensations is an administrative not a legislative act: that it is a decision how and where and to what extent to apply or enforce laws, in the light of particular circumstances. It is the work, therefore, not of the legislator necessarily but of an executive officer. And that it is the province of the bishop in his diocese to apply and administer the law scarcely admits of doubt. But however this may be, the fact remains that from early times the bishops had dispensed, and that their loss of this independent power to the Pope in the Church of Rome is a relatively modern development. In the Orthodox Church of the East the bishops exercise a similar power of "economy" under the supervising authority of provincial and general councils.

Again, even if we accept the maxim, the question remains what is the legislative authority in the Church. And we may hold (1) that authority in each diocese is the bishop—acting, no doubt, after consultation with his clergy and with the general assent of the laity: and (2) that bishops exercise this authority after joint discussion and agreement among themselves in Councils. Consequently the proper authority to grant a dispensation is the Diocesan Bishop: but he will exercise his authority in accordance with decisions agreed upon by him and his brother bishops. They will consult together and decide from what laws and for what sort of reasons a dispensation shall be granted. And any doubtful but important case they will refer to their joint consideration.

The existence of some such dispensing power, vested in the bishop, is essential if the canon law is to retain that element of flexibility which is necessary to its true nature and to the attainment of its purpose. This dispensing power has its administrative counterpart in the device of "toleration". In most branches of law the administrative and executive officers have no option but to enforce the law wherever they find that it is being disobeyed. With canon law it is different. The authority of the bishop is such that he can, if he thinks fit, overlook and take no sort of action against even open and notorious breaches of the law. It is in this way that customs which are contrary to the law are able to develop.

Such a custom may be one which, though technically against the law, the authority thinks is a harmless or even a good custom, well suited to the peculiar needs or character of a particular local church. In that case, the authority is glad to take no action. A formal dispensation to allow the practice is not granted, perhaps because it is not asked for, perhaps because the authority is not prepared to grant that amount of explicit permission, lest it should serve, maybe, as an encouragement to its adoption in other places where there is less justification. On the other hand, the custom may be one of which authority thoroughly disapproves, yet which for grave reasons it is reluctant to oppose openly. For example,

it may be morally certain that an attempt to enforce the law would not be followed by obedience, but by persistent and open disobedience—that the attempt would provoke contumacy. This would end at worst in schism, at best in the prolonged excommunication of some individuals who are acting in entire good faith, being convinced that it is their duty not to abandon the practice which has been forbidden. For reasons of this kind authority may be moved to tolerate, at least for a time, a disobedience to the law of which it disapproves. It hopes in this way to avoid schism: it hopes that in time the practice will cease of its own accord.

And this brings me to my last point—the treatment of offences and the character of ecclesiastical punishment. An ecclesiastical punishment ought not, strictly speaking, to have about it any element of "vindictive" punishment. In other branches of law an offence is held to merit or deserve some punishment by the payment of which "the offended majesty of the law" is re-established. In ecclesiastical law it is not so, or should not be so. The infliction of an ecclesiastical punishment has only two purposes. Either it seeks the correction or reform of the offender or it seeks to demonstrate publicly that certain things are, beyond any contradiction, against the law; or it seeks both.

In so far as it seeks the former, the punishment comes to an end when the offender shows penitence and promises amendment of life. Suppose that a priest is inhibited for practising simony or preaching heresy. The inhibition should be removed as soon as he promises not to preach heresy any more or not to practise simony. He may, it is true, be kept for a further period under discipline—he may be sent to a college to study orthodoxy or put under the charge of another priest in his pastoral work—but that is not a punishment for his past offence; it is a precautionary training for the future exercise of his ministry. Particularly should this be true of the supreme ecclesiastical punishment, excommunication. The purpose of excommunication, in so far as it concerns the sinner, is to awaken him to a consciousness of the enor-

mity of his sin. To declare him outcast from the Christian Community, or to deprive him of sacramental grace is the most dramatic assertion possible that the sin in which he persists without repentance is offensive to God and totally incompatible with his Christian profession. But it is a sin in which he persists without repentance. If he repents and resolves to cease from the sin, the divine forgiveness is immediate and the sinner's salvation and actual amendment of life imperatively demand his restoration to his place within the Christian Community and his admission to the Sacraments.

It is obvious that the sin which is held to merit excommunication may be committed in good faith or in bad faith. If it is committed in bad faith, authority must carefully consider whether excommunication is likely to achieve its end of shocking the conscience into repentance, or whether it will only confirm a spirit of obstinacy and guilty rebellion and result in contumacy. If the latter is the more likely, it may be right to accept the danger to the sinner of receiving the Sacraments in a state of conscious sin, in the hope that the continued life within the Christian Community may of itself, in time, effect a reformation. The presumption, however, is in favour of excommunication. If the sin be committed in good faith, excommunication is unlikely to prove an effective remedy. It will perhaps cause the sinner carefully to consider all over again his reasons for disobeying the law: it will convince him, if he were not already convinced, of the deep importance which the Church attaches to the observance of this law. It can scarcely do more. It carries also this danger, that it may induce him to abandon a course of action which he still believes in conscience to be his duty: in other words, it may induce him to exchange a material sin for a formal one. In general it may be said that the excommunication of a sinner who is in good faith is to be deprecated in so far as it concerns the good of the sinner himself. The presumption here is against excommunication.

But of course there is also the good of the Church to be considered. The sin may be such that it is impossible for

authority to take no action without at the same time en-
couraging others to commit it. To excommunicate the sinner,
in however good faith he is, may be the only way of declaring
effectively that what he persists in doing is in fact a sin. If he
is not excommunicated, but continues to live publicly as a
member of the Church, his example may come to be widely
followed. Others may say to themselves that this thing is
apparently permitted, that therefore it is presumably not
wrong, that therefore they may do it too. Thus the good of
the Church as a whole and the purity of her ethical teaching
may require the excommunication of one who is himself not
consciously—as he sees it—doing anything wrong at all.

Yet excommunication is a perilous weapon, to be used
with exquisite discretion and as a last resort, but on occasion
to be used fearlessly. Here are two possible examples— The
man who has divorced his wife and in all good faith married
again: is it possible not to excommunicate him and not, at
the same time, to encourage a general opinion that divorce
and remarriage is permissible? The man who conscientiously
believes that it is possible to belong to the Communist Party
without subscribing to its atheism, and that social justice
requires that he should do so: is it possible not to excommunicate him and not, at the same time, to encourage a general
opinion that membership of a confessed and militantly
atheistic association is compatible with Christianity? Does
the good of the Church demand excommunication in these
cases, in spite of the absence of wilful sin?

It is, I say, a case for exquisite discretion. Excommunication generally is not likely to reform the sinner; it is more
likely to harm him. Before, therefore, it is pronounced,
authority should be convinced that the good of the Church
demands it. It is for this reason that "absence of any danger
of scandal"—i.e. the fact that nobody, or practically nobody
knows about the sin—is often held, and rightly held, to be
a sufficient ground for toleration and for not excommunicat-
ing where the sinner is in good faith. For if, and so long as,
the offence is secret it sets no bad example. Therefore the

good of the Church cannot be said to demand excommunication. Indeed, perhaps the reverse, since excommunication would make public what is so far secret. The point is that no ecclesiastical punishment, least of all that of excommunication, may ever be purely vindictive; it does not aim at punishment, it must seek the good of either Church or sinner. To flexibility in making and adapting laws is thus added a flexibility in their application and enforcement.

The canon law should at all times express the common mind of the Church of any time and place. It should express on the one hand her understanding of God's Law, with its necessary implications for Christian behaviour and its necessary requirements for the Ordering of Church Sacraments: this is the immutable part of the canon law. It should also express the common mind of the Church on all such matters as require regulation but which may properly vary from age to age or place to place: this is the mutable part of the law. And individual canons take different forms as they refer to one part or the other, and in accordance with the importance which the common mind of the Church attaches to particular matters. Thus some canons are couched in the imperative, and by their very form make it clear that no exceptions can be allowed. Others, though expressed in the imperative, assert or imply that for sufficient reason there may be exceptions, but such exceptions must be authoritatively permitted. Yet others are expressed in the optative—"It is desirable that . . ." "A minister should, unless reasonably let or hindered . . ." and so on. These carry the implication that in all ordinary circumstances the Church holds that this or that should be done, or should be done in this or that way, but that each man has freedom to act differently without further permission if in his serious judgement the circumstances are sufficiently out of the ordinary to justify a deviation.

The canons are the norms and standards of Christian behaviour. They are the expression of that which is recognised by the generality of Christians as either necessary or conducive to the well-being of the Church and the salvation

of souls. They command obedience—but the reasoned obedience of a good conscience. They have but one purpose—to keep the Church from evil and to prescribe what is necessary or useful to the living of the life which is hid with Christ in God. In imposing them the Church speaks with the authority of the Body of Christ and under the inspiration of the Holy Spirit Who dwells in all her members. In enforcing them she seeks to follow His example of Whom it is written, "A bruised reed shall he not break and smoking flax shall he not quench."

BIBLIOGRAPHY

AYLIFFE, John, *Parergon Juris Canonici Anglicani: or, A Commentary by Way of Supplement to the Canons and Constitutions of the Church of England.* London, 1726.

BRYS, J., *De Dispensatione in Jure Canonico.* Lowain, 1925.

BURN, Richard, *Ecclesiastical Law.* 4 vols. 2nd ed. London, 1767.

CARDWELL, Edward, *Documentary Annals of the Church of England.* 2 vols. Oxford, 1839.

Synodalia, A Collection of Articles of Religion, Canons and Proceedings of Convocations in the Province of Canterbury, from the Year 1547 to the Year 1717. 2 vols. Oxford, 1842.

The Reformation of the Ecclesiastical Law as attempted in the Reigns of King Henry VIII, King Edward VI, and Queen Elizabeth. Oxford, 1850.

CIMETIER, F., *Les Sources du Droit Canonique.* Paris, 1930.

CRIPPS, Henry William, *A Practical Treatise on the Law relating to the Church and Clergy.* 8th ed. London, 1937.

DAVIS, H. W. C., *The Canon Law in England, in Henry William Carless Davis, 1874–1928.*

FOURNIER, Paul, and LE BRAS, Gabriel, *Histoire des Collections Canoniques en Occident.* 2 vols. Paris, 1931.

GIBSON, Edmund, *Codex Juris Ecclesiastici Anglicani.* 2 vols. 2nd ed. Oxford, 1761.

GODOLPHIN, John, *Repertorium Canonicum: or, an Abridgement of the Ecclesiastical Laws of the Realm, etc.* 3rd ed. London, 1687.

HINSCHIUS, Paul, *Decretales Pseudo-Isidorianae.* 1863.

JOHNSON, John, *The Clergyman's Vade-Mecum; or an Account of the Ancient and Present Church of England, etc.* 2 parts. London, 1709.

A Collection of the Laws and Canons of the Church of England, From its First Foundation to the Conquest, and From the Conquest to the Reign of King Henry VIII. Translated into English with Explanatory Notes. 2 vols. Oxford, 1850.

JOYCE, James Wayland, *England's Sacred Synods. A Constitutional History of the Convocations of the Clergy, from the Earliest Records of Christianity in Britain to the Date of the Promulgation of the Present Book of Common Prayer.* London, 1855.

LYNWOOD, William, *Provinciale (seu Constitutiones Angliae).* Oxford, 1679

MAASSEN, F., *Geschichte der Quellen und der Literatur der Canonischen Rechts im Abendlande bis zum Anganges der Mittelalturs.*

MCNEILL and GAMER, *Medieval Handbooks of Penance.* Columbia University, 1938.

MAITLAND, F. W., *Roman Canon Law in the Church of England.* London, 1898.

MAKOWER, Felix, *The Constitutional History and Constitution of the Church of England.* London, 1895.

OUGHTON, Thomas, *Ordo Judicorum: sive Methodus Procedendi in Negotiis et Litibus in Foro Ecclesiastico-Civili Britannico et Hibernico.* 2 vols. London, 1718.

PHILLIMORE, Sir Robert Joseph, *The Practice and Courts of Civil and Ecclesiastical Law.* London, 1848.
The Ecclesiastical Law of the Church of England. 2 vols. 2nd ed. London, 1895.

POWICKE, F. M., *The Early History of Canon Law,* in *History, XVIII.* 11–19.

REPORT OF THE ARCHBISHOPS' COMMISSION ON CANON LAW, *The Canon Law of the Church of England.* S.P.C.K., London, 1947.

SHARP, Thomas, *The Rubric in the Book of Common Prayer and the Canons of the Church of England, so far as they relate to the Parochial Clergy, considered in a Course of Visitation Charges.* London, 1753.

TURNER, C. H., *The Organization of the Church. Cambridge Medieval History,* Vol. I, c. VI.

WATSON, William, *The Clergyman's Law; or, The Complete Incumbent.* 3rd ed. London, 1725.

WOOD, Edmund G., *The Regal Power of the Church; or, The Fundamentals of the Canon Law. A Dissertation.* Cambridge, 1888.